What People Are Saying...

"When I first encountered Diane and began to learn about her marriage, I was astonished. That someone could be suffering so much, yet not waver in her commitment to her marriage...what a contrast to how quickly most people marry and divorce in our culture. Diane's dedication to learn new ways of thinking about relating, and every moment of courage it took to implement them, are truly inspiring. And now I am moved by her generosity in sharing the journey, insights, challenges, and victories with others. If, even in hopelessness, you have a fraction of her determination, you can benefit immensely from her book."

~ Alison A. Armstrong, The Queen's Code.
Creator and Co-Founder PAX Programs Incorporated.

———————◆◇◆———————

"As a preschool teacher for 34 years and a parent coach, I've seen firsthand how much stronger relationships become when we genuinely listen to under-stand. Don't Let Misunderstanding Win *perfectly captures this truth.*

One day, a preschooler in my care was riding his tricycle with a toy truck and chalk in the back basket. Suddenly, he stopped, dumped the chalk on the ground, and rode off. I asked him to pick it up for safety—he got upset. I gave him space, and minutes later, he came back with a bucket, gathered the chalk, and happily rode away.

When I asked why he was upset, he said, "My truck was getting chalk on the wheels." That simple moment reminded me: when we pause and listen, we uncover the real reason behind actions, and sometimes, we discover a thoughtful problem-solver in the making.

There is so much information in this book, yet it's easy to follow. The prompts at the end of each chapter make it simple to apply the ideas in your own life. This book is a valuable guide for shifting our perspective from what we want to what matters to the person in front of us. It's an enjoyable, practical read that can truly make us better parents, teachers, and partners.

~ Ruth Maille, Owner & CEO, Stumbling Blocks Preschool.

Don't Let Misunderstanding Win *is a heartfelt and practical guide for anyone who wants to experience more harmony and connection in their relationships. Diane doesn't just offer theory—she shares hard-won insights from her own life and thorough research, showing how small shifts in perspective can lead to big changes in how we communicate and connect. The questions she includes after each chapter were thought-provoking and reinforced the concepts she teaches. Her words empowered me to see beyond my assumptions and understand the unique motivations of the people in my life. I feel better equipped to respond in ways that heal, restore, and strengthen those bonds. This is a book you'll be referencing again and again. I know I will!*

~ Kelly Williams Hale. Speaker, Author, Mentor, @thebebravelife

Don't Let Misunderstanding Win

Cultivate Better Responses & Results Across the Spectrum of Relationships

Diane Lawbaugh

Don't Let Misunderstanding Win:
Cultivate Better Responses & Results Across the Spectrum of Relationships

Copyright ©2025 Diane Lawbaugh

Published by World Publishing and Productions
PO Box 8722, Jupiter, FL 33468
Worldpublishingandproductions.com

ISBN: 978-1-957111-54-4

Library of Congress Control Number: 2025921615

Acknowledgments

My deepest appreciation to my husband. His belief in me, steadfast love through good and bad times, and permission to share so much of our story made this book possible.

To my dear friend, Kristine. Thank you for your living example of how this information changed your life, and your insistence that I go to my first class.

To the team at World Publishing and Productions. My thanks for believing in this message and partnering with me. Julie, thank you for your countless hours and incredible editing skills. Kelly, thank you for your patience and beautiful design of the cover. Kimberly, thank you for your continual encouragement throughout the process.

To Alison Armstrong, her team, and my colleagues in the 2018 PAX Mastery and Certification program. Thank you, Alison, for your passion to create the courses that changed my reality. Thank you for your encouragement to make the material my own and share it with the world. To the PAX support team, thank you for your patience with my endless questions. To my 2018 colleagues, thank you for your curiosity, courage, and openness to participate and share during our journey together.

To the men and women who engaged in my research panel. Thank you for your time and vulnerability. Your contributions verified the truth and consistency of what I learned in my courses.

Contents

Introduction

Have you ever finished a conversation feeling beat up and wondering what happened? You are not alone if you can relate. Be encouraged—you hold in your hands a treasure trove of information that has the power to make your life better, all centered around some great news:

Misunderstanding doesn't have to win.

Misunderstanding beat up my husband and me for years. Growing like a stalactite, it continued to drip into our marriage to the point that the sharp, jagged edges created raw spots within each of our souls. As a result, we were hurting one another nearly every day. Individually, we both knew we loved each other, which made it even more perplexing that the pain in our lives continued to become a bigger and bigger obstacle. Why was this happening? *How* was this happening?

Desperation and hopelessness were getting a stranglehold on me. I had no answers. Witnessing other relationships like ours sabotaged me into believing that living in this painful way was inevitable.[1] Marriage seemed to be an unsolvable problem with two flavors of distress to choose from—the anguish of staying together or the torture of divorce.

Thankfully, that perspective proved untrue.

---

1. Gray/Grey Divorce

Diving into my questions, I invested over 1,300 hours in training, research, and test teaching. I conducted 75% of my research with men from five to eighty-nine years old and 25% with women from their early twenties to late sixties, plus utilized my first-hand resource of being a woman. Despite the diversity of my subjects, the consistent findings I discovered were astounding and convincing; they allowed me to view my husband and myself through a new lens.

I invite you to share in these discoveries that have changed the overall condition of my life for the better. Explore these revelations and uncover a new awareness across your spectrum of relationships that will result in a better quality of life and the illumination of new points of view.

As you go through this book, you will experience change by simply applying what you read. However, consciously connecting this content with your own life and experiences will enable you to retain much more of this life-altering information and see an even greater outcome. I encourage you to exercise curiosity about these teachings and use them to look deeper into yourself and the people around you. Although the basic principles remain consistent, your experience with each person will most likely vary because we all have unique qualities. Regardless, you will be delightfully surprised at what is possible in your interactions.

For example, before knowing this material, I was very good at judging people for what I believed they *should* be giving me, rather than appreciating what they were contributing to me. Unfortunately, I excelled at this for years, especially when interacting with my husband. With the benefit of hindsight, I see my motivation came from my desire to be "perfect." My criticisms, therefore, stemmed from *assuming* my husband also wanted to be perfect. I was "simply helping him see" where he needed to work on that perfection. YIKES! Does anyone want to be treated this way?

As I dug deeper, I discovered that there is a significant difference in what drives women and men. Listen to women speak and notice how often they use the word "perfect"—about anything and everything. By using perfection as their measuring stick, women set themselves up to fail. However, most men want to be the best version of themselves. Listen to how men speak: "I want to be a *better* man." That is an achievable goal, one they can win at. I am so thankful that men have taught me this valuable lesson!!

As you read, don't be startled if thoughts come into your mind, such as, *Can this be true?* and *How can this be possible?* This is a good thing! Use these thoughts to go deeper. Be curious and try out these new perspectives.

If you are ready to defeat misunderstanding and create better responses and results across the spectrum of your relationships, let's start our adventure together!

Section 1

The Power of Clarity

Have you heard the old Indian parable about a group of blind men who come across an elephant for the first time? Each touches a different part of the animal in an attempt to learn about it and comes to a conclusion based solely on his experience. Because each man only believes what he has directly encountered, two things happen. First, they all have a distorted perspective of what an elephant is. Second, each individual mistrusts what the others say because it contradicts "the truth" concluded from the facts personally collected.

To the best of our knowledge, this parable has existed since approximately 500 BC. That tells me that a lack of clarity about our perceptions and interactions has been creating misunderstandings for a very long time!

I used to be "blind" when it came to understanding the men around me, unable to see the whole picture clearly. Since I am a woman and had not yet looked beyond my own line of sight, my sole reference point was how women experience the world. I was convinced that "my facts" were "the truth." I distrusted what men would tell me because what they said often contradicted "my facts."

The definition of clarity is the degree to which we perceive or understand something as it truly is, with freedom from indistinctness or ambiguity. What a difference I experienced when I discovered how distorted and unclear my lens was. You know that feeling when you get new glasses and you realize how much you've not been able to see? Yup, that was me.

There is no better place to start dismantling misunderstandings between men and women than gaining clarity about our differences.

Chapter One

Six Essentials for Better Relationships

Whether you are interacting with a romantic partner, business partner, parents, siblings, children, or friends, understanding these six essentials will help provide you with new lenses to see our world and experience better responses and results:

1. Different Is Not Bad
2. Choose to Live from Scarcity or Abundance
3. Operating Systems
4. Worth-It Calculation
5. Listening to Learn
6. Look for Clark Kent

Essential #1 - Different Is Not Bad

I must admit my surprise when I realized how much guacamole had to teach me about relationships. Curious?

Think about it. Both avocados and limes are green. Both are fruits. Both have seeds. However, biting into a lime and expecting it to taste like an avocado would, at the least, surprise you. The sour might even frustrate or anger you because the flavor didn't live up to your expectations. And yet, if you appreciate the differences between these two fruits and mix them together, the uniqueness of each complements the other, resulting in something pretty darn tasty. At least, I'm a big fan of guacamole!

How many times do we apply similar logic to the people around us?

We are all humans. We all need oxygen, water, food, and shelter to stay alive. Therefore, our *expectations* tend to be that the person next to us *should* act and respond to a given circumstance the same way we would. My experience, however, is that expectation and reality rarely match, particularly when interacting with the opposite gender.

If you are a woman, I'm guessing the thought, *A woman wouldn't act that way,* has crossed your mind many times when dealing with men. Men tend to think similarly about women. You know what? Both responses are absolutely correct. But can you see the problem? When this is our mindset, we tend to judge others who react differently as "misbehaving." **When we judge, we label. When we label, the person before us stops being a multi-faceted, amazing creation and instead becomes a "thing" we must control to get what we want.**

I was quite surprised to discover that, unbeknownst to me, the label I'd created for my husband was "a big, hairy, misbehaving woman." My actions and our marriage definitely reflected my viewpoint. However, as I've grown in my ability to see my husband more and more clearly for the man he is, my demeanor, words, and actions have become less adversarial and judgmental. He no longer has to defend himself from my behavior. This dynamic alone has absolutely changed how we interact with one another for the better!

When we interact with others, whether it be with people of our same or opposite sex, we can never assume their reactions will match the way we would behave. Regardless of how many similarities we may share, we have just as many—or more!—different life experiences that impact the uniqueness of our reactions.

So, how do we begin changing this cycle of misunderstanding, judgment, frustration, and hurting one another? The good news is that it's pretty simple to get started.

Equip yourself with these three questions that you can always use to help you see other people more clearly.

What if no one is misbehaving?
What if we are misunderstanding one another?
What if there is a good reason for that response, action, behavior, or point of view?

Being aware of and answering these questions can help us recognize that the person in front of us has unique attributes. Further, it can allow us to appreciate our differences and find ways to complement one another—just like limes and avocados—creating better responses, results, and relationships across the spectrum of our lives.

Here's a word of warning: There is no point in asking yourself these questions if you are not willing to consider changing your point of view.

Did that sentence cause you to feel some resistance to reading any further? Don't worry if it did. That's a pretty natural response. I'd encourage you to walk right through that friction and read on.

I haven't met anyone yet who has not been hurt at some point by the opposite gender. Because of that, a common reaction to the information in this book is: *Why should I change for someone else?* Actually, by suggesting you be open to adopting a new viewpoint, I'm giving you an opportunity to honor yourself first. This is about helping you enhance the quality of *your* life. Seriously.

Obviously, there are millions of lenses through which we can view circumstances. For our purposes, let's focus on three of them. We drink from our perspectives every day—so let's imagine them in three wine glasses.

The first glass is filled with doing the same thing(s) over and over, while expecting a different result. If you look in the dictionary, that is the literal definition of insanity. This approach is more common than you might think—a few examples might be how we approach what we eat, how much we exercise, how much sleep we get, and how we treat others in our relationships.

The second glass is filled with bitterness and pain. Wrapped around the stem of this glass is a chain. What if the thing we do over and over is drink from our bitterness and pain to prove to ourselves, and maybe others, that we can protect ourselves by holding on to our pain? Or what if we think that holding on to our pain will hurt the person who hurt us? For your consideration, drinking from this cup was described to me by Dr. Mario Rivera this way: "Bitterness is like drinking a glass of poison and hoping it kills the person sitting next to you." Not exactly protecting or honoring yourself, is it? Instead, drinking from this cup actually imprisons you.

The third glass is filled with forgiveness. Choosing to drink from this cup sets you free from drinking insanity, bitterness, and pain—creating space within you to receive healing. Sounds like a good idea to me! You can choose to:

- Forgive others for hurting you—no longer allowing yourself to be chained to that pain. Forgiving someone doesn't mean that what they did wasn't wrong; it means you are severing your connection from the pain they caused.

- Forgive yourself for repeatedly drinking from the cups of insanity, bitterness, and pain, or for repeating any hurtful pattern, because you just didn't know any better.

For me, forgiveness looks like recognizing which of my thoughts and actions are a poisonous cocktail and then choosing to stop drinking it and even let go of the cup. When I do this, I experience a chaser shot of healing and freedom. As you move forward with what is illuminated for you in this book, you can choose your point of view and drink in healing and empowerment for a life of freedom.

Everything in this book has been written to help you drink from the third glass. Each moment is always your choice and no one else's.

Essential #2 - Choose to Live from Scarcity or Abundance

You wake up in the middle of the night and start walking to the bathroom. BOOM! You stub your toe. How quickly and intensely do you respond? There's a good chance it is not PG-rated, right? These are your instincts at work. They are quicker than cognitive thought and come directly from our hard-wired survival system, which is a very good thing to have. To get technical, our instincts are a primal, biological urge that compels us to take action to relieve tension. I call this part of us Human Raw.

Instincts become problematic when they run unchecked in our lives., They are triggered by threats—*Danger, Danger*—and, surprisingly, opportunities. It takes very little time for *Ooooh, opportunity!* to be swallowed up by doubts that feel threatening as our thoughts turn to *Uh-oh, what if I blow it?*

We can recognize that our instincts are at work by the tension in our bodies. At the bottom line, the perceived need to solve the problem of survival creates tension: *How do I outlast you? Survive?* There is intense energy within our instinctual responses. The compulsions they generate cause us to form survival strategies that turn men and women into adversaries.

Can you see where that could create all sorts of problems in our interactions?

The good news is that life can be better than this. Besides our Human Raw, we have two other built-in capacities to help us—our Soul Processes and Human Spirit. Let's look at the characteristics of these three.

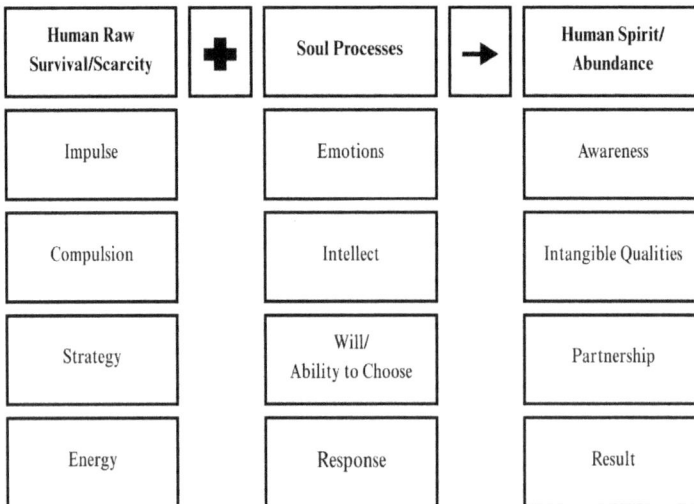

Human Raw Survival/Scarcity	✚	Soul Processes	→	Human Spirit/ Abundance
Impulse		Emotions		Awareness
Compulsion		Intellect		Intangible Qualities
Strategy		Will/ Ability to Choose		Partnership
Energy		Response		Result

Rather than trying to control or suppress the natural energy that our Human Raw state is known for—our survival traits—we can put that energy to good use by applying our Soul Processes. When we respond to outside influences by adding emotions, intellect, and will, we can live from the abundance of our Human Spirit. Living from the Human Spirit is possible by becoming aware of the material provided in this book and mixing in intangible qualities such as curiosity, compassion, and understanding. We use these Human Spirit components to partner with ourselves and the people around us. The final result is the ability to live from a place of abundance rather than being restricted by a scarcity, survival mindset.

A beautiful example of what's possible when all three parts of us work in tandem was shared with me by my client, Mary.

For most of her life, Mary was led by her instincts, which resulted in her constantly checking for people's responses to her. Mary experienced high levels of tension most of the time. Her instincts caused her to be continually aware of whether the people around her were happy with her and liked her. If Mary detected they weren't, she would try to modify herself or her actions so they would be pleased with her. The problem with her modus operandi was that altering herself never satisfied Mary because she was not being true to herself.

After several coaching sessions, Mary shared that she had recently started feeling tension about a relationship. Instead of reacting to her desire to be liked on the Human Raw level by trying to morph herself, she chose to add the Soul Processes—her will, intellect, and emotions—into her decision-making. She suddenly became aware of the HUGE price she pays when she modifies herself.

Mary partnered her new awareness—her Human Spirit—with the intangible, spiritual qualities of revelation, understanding, and compassion for herself! She had learned the importance of honoring herself rather than altering herself, allowing her to move from living with tension, survival, and scarcity to living with peace, thriving, and abundance. Mary told me, "Here's to learning how to choose myself over and over and over again!"

Are you interested in learning how you can live your daily life out of the abundance of your Human Spirit? Ok! Let's build a little more foundation to help you.

Essential #3 - Operating Systems

Surprise! Computers, tablets, and smartphones are not the only things with unique operating systems.

People have two very distinct operating systems: Hunting Mode and Gathering Mode. Both men and women can operate in either, and neither is better than the other—they are simply different. You can think of it like iPhones and Androids. You can text, make phone calls, have a video conference, or take pictures using either one, but the internal processes on those devices are quite different.

First, let's take a look at the most common default operating mode for men and women. Of course, there will be exceptions because none of us is exactly alike.

For men, the default is Hunting Mode. Men have higher levels of testosterone, which provides necessary fuel for the intense, goal-oriented, single-focus that happens during Hunting Mode. You will see men in Gathering Mode only when they are at play—when no specific results are necessary. Notice I said "play." Think of a dad playing with his children, which differs significantly from a dad participating in or training his child at a sport; both these activities involve specific, definite goals.

A woman's naturally higher estrogen level makes Gathering her default operating mode. Moreover, estrogen provides fuel for women to switch between Gathering and Hunting *very quickly!* This quick shifting between the two modes can sometimes confuse both the men and women around us!! After we delve more into the specific attributes of each mode, I'll share a story from one of my clients, which will bring more clarity about this shift.

Use this information to alter your awareness. Look for the two modes in your own experiences at work and home as we review these attributes. Use the five attributes listed below to help identify Hunting and Gathering Modes.

ATTRIBUTE: FOCUS

In Hunting Mode, focus is concentrated on a single goal. Please don't confuse a goal with a task. For example, a football coach has the goal of winning the game. That goal is comprised of multiple components, including training the offense, defense, and special teams. It is important to note that in Hunting Mode, we *naturally* screen out any detail that is irrelevant to the current goal.

An example of this in our day-to-day lives is when we focus on a deadline at work. You can be so ingrained in your work that someone may walk up and startle you—you screen out their approach without consciously thinking about it. As I mentioned earlier, men's higher levels of testosterone tend to put them in single-focus most of the time. This means that, without even realizing it, they screen out details that are irrelevant to their current goal *most of the time.* How often have you misunderstood single-focus—in either male *or* female hunters—as a personal insult? Repeat after me: IT'S NOT PERSONAL.

In Gathering Mode, focus takes the form of diffuse awareness, because every detail is essential. This is easier to comprehend if we look back to when hunting and gathering were, literally, how we survived. If you were gathering food for your tribe, your instincts compelled you to notice and collect details such as which meadow had berries that were ripe, which one would have fruit soon, whether poisonous plants surrounded the berries, and whether animal tracks were present that could indicate danger. These details were the difference between life and death. What does this have to do with the present day? It's important to remember that even as much as humans have evolved, these instincts still impact us quicker than cognitive thought.

My husband and I now have language for when I start sharing voluminous details he does not need. He'll look at me and say, "No berries, please." This makes us both laugh, and it works far better than him becoming frustrated, cutting me off, and me feeling disrespected and hurt because he didn't value the details I was meticulously sharing. Can you see it?

My client, Debbie, is a professional author who works out of her home. After learning this information, she gasped deeply. I asked her if she was OK. Debbie shared that she now understands and has language for what happens when she is interrupted by her daughter. This teaching helped Debbie recognize that her daughter never knows which mode she will encounter when she knocks on her mother's door. When her daughter—all excited about the details she wants to share—interrupts hunter-mommy, Debbie often snaps at her. During her work hours, the professional author exhibits very different behavior than gatherer-mommy, who loves to sit on the bed with her daughter, taking in every detail of her adventures. Debbie told me, "The poor child has had two parents in one body!"

Does this real-life example help you see that being aware of these modes and how quickly women can switch between them is essential to achieving better responses, results, and relationships? Debbie's story powerfully demonstrates how easily misunderstandings occur with the people in our lives if we and they are unaware of operating modes.

ATTRIBUTE: MINDSET

In Hunting Mode, having single-focus creates a committed mindset to achieving the goal.

In Gathering Mode, diffuse awareness sets the stage for the mindset to be uncommitted and open to all the possibilities that continue to present themselves as more details are gathered.

Being alert to this particular attribute and the way it presents itself has eliminated the persistent fights that popped up quite frequently between my husband and me when we went out for dinner. Before we left the house, we would select where we wanted to go, for example, Jason's for soup and salad. I had no clue my husband now had a goal to achieve—get us successfully to Jason's! His single-focus was definitely ignited. However, while he was driving, my diffuse awareness would kick in, and I'd notice another restaurant with nice salads. I'd say something like, "Oh, I just saw Logan's. Would you rather go there for a salad?"

My single-focused, committed husband was suddenly quite frustrated with me. I had no idea why. I thought I was being flexible and helpful to mention the second restaurant as a possibility. My husband's thoughts were more along the lines of, *Wait. I thought the goal was Jason's. Are we changing the goal? What's going on here? What am I supposed to be accomplishing?*

Neither of us was misbehaving, but we certainly were hurting one another because we were misunderstanding each other.

ATTRIBUTE: HOW YOU LISTEN

Those in Hunting Mode and those in Gathering Mode have very distinct differences in how they approach conversations.

For people in Hunting Mode, the most important thing is to know either the point or the problem so they can successfully achieve the goal.

People in Gathering Mode listen to discern whether they agree or disagree with the details they are gathering in the conversation. The instinct driving this approach is that these individuals feel connected and safe if they agree. They feel disconnected and unsafe if they disagree.

This leads us directly to the fourth attribute.

ATTRIBUTE: HOW SAFETY IS EXPERIENCED

The uniqueness of how safety is experienced in either operating mode is definitely impacted by whether a person is estrogen-based or testosterone-based.

When you combine being estrogen-based with Gathering Mode, a woman who receives positive attention and interest feels safe knowing the person providing those things is connected to her. Modern women are still very aware at an instinctual level of their vulnerability when they feel disconnected from those around them. They experience this as a very uncomfortable, anxious, agitated feeling in the middle of their chest.

If you are having trouble relating to this concept, ladies, think about how you feel when you do not receive a response to a text. Need I say more? The nickname my teachers used for this was "Tiger Bait." Again, it happens quicker than cognitive thought. This instinct ties back to when we were living in tribes. When a tiger or a marauder attack would happen, it was a reality that females would not be protected if they were not well-connected to the people around them.

When in Hunting Mode, the experience of safety occurs when producing a result. This instinct ties back to hunters needing to successfully deliver the results of procreating, protecting the tribe from an adversary, or providing food, shelter, and clothing for survival. Respect and trust were key elements in producing these results.

In today's world, this still happens for both men and women in Hunting Mode. Think about when you have a specific goal to achieve. You need to be able to trust and respect the people on your team and also have their respect and trust, correct? This is not so different from ancient days and literal hunts. Only the individuals who had proven they could be relied upon not to turn and run when faced with a marauder or large beast of prey were respected enough to be invited and allowed to participate in the hunt. Men's inherently higher testosterone levels predispose them to Hunting Mode the majority of the time, making the need to give and receive trust and respect that much more intense and frequent for them.

ATTRIBUTE: WHAT MAKES SOMETHING "WORTH IT"

In Gathering Mode, the experience of something being "Worth-It" comes when it can be checked off as done. How many of you use written or mental checklists? This is a direct result of the diffuse awareness that is part of Gathering Mode. Being so aware of all the details around us causes every minutia to natter at us. Crooked pillows say, "Straighten me." Dust bunnies shout, "Clean me." An empty fridge yells, "Fill me." Gentlemen, this may help you understand why your wife wants to clean her way out of the house when you leave for vacation. She doesn't want the details of undone tasks going with her! The way women quiet their environment is to get things done. The prize of peacefulness is won when details are silenced. Definitely worth it.

This awareness of details is why socks on the floor or dishes in the sink speak to most women most of the time. Whereas most men, most of the time, don't even see the socks or dishes due to their tendency to be single-focused on their current goal. Socks and dishes are simply not relevant. Does this concept help you see and understand how the action of someone walking past these items IS NOT PERSONAL??? Without understanding the impact of operating modes, this type of situation can easily spark a fight.

In Hunting Mode, the prize of an activity being Worth-It is won when a person experiences a greater return than the investment of time, energy, and money and/or resources used to achieve the goal. This also ties back to the survival instinct. Ancient hunters were very aware that if you used up more of your time, energy, or resources (arrows, food) than you got back from the hunt, you would die—which definitely made the trip NOT Worth-It. In its simplest form, this is an unconscious point system constantly at play within someone in Hunting Mode. You win by getting the most points possible. This element is such a driving force of Hunting

Mode that understanding it is the fourth essential to establish better responses, results, and relationships, which we will study separately.

Before we move on to that discussion, let's return to the illustration of my husband and me heading to dinner, now applying our new awareness of the two operating modes and their attributes to the disconnect between my husband's Hunting Mode and my Gathering Mode.

Instincts were at play in my husband to successfully produce the result of getting us to dinner at the restaurant we'd chosen initially. For him, at an unconscious level, this meant we would be safe and survive. Very important! Overlay this with the priority of investing his time, energy, and money in such a way that he would win at accomplishing a greater return than what he was investing. Suddenly, his intensity to know and achieve the goal becomes very understandable.

Instincts were at play in me to ensure my husband was aware of the new possibilities available to us because of the details I'd collected during our drive. Instinctual tension within me made it seem imperative that he know all our dining possibilities in case the first one didn't work out. The frustration he voiced to me as I provided "berries" he didn't deem relevant made me feel unsafe because it was the exact opposite of positive attention and interest. This disconnect threw me into survival mode. With that frame of mind, I became adversarial, which also triggered him to become adversarial.

This downward spiral is insidious, yet it occurs quicker than cognitive thought. We were completely unaware of what was happening and why it was happening. Therefore, this scenario repeated itself over and over. This is just one way the stalactite of pain continued to drip into our lives.

Now, I choose to hold the details I collect of possible alternatives until we arrive at our destination and find out if we actually need them. This way, we both win, and the time we share is much more enjoyable.

Essential #4 - Worth-It Calculation

You may be surprised how much you will encounter the Worth-It Calculation when interacting with those in Hunting Mode. During my research, I asked a 40-year-old man if the Worth-It Calculation continues as a barometer throughout the process of achieving a goal. He said, "Oh, I see it, and I think it happens subconsciously."

The entire calculation is depicted below. We will review each part separately.

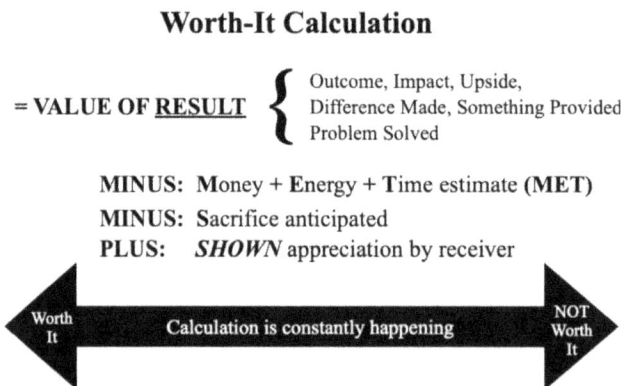

Worth-It Calculation

$$= \textbf{VALUE OF \underline{RESULT}} \begin{cases} \text{Outcome, Impact, Upside,} \\ \text{Difference Made, Something Provided} \\ \text{Problem Solved} \end{cases}$$

MINUS: Money + Energy + Time estimate **(MET)**
MINUS: Sacrifice anticipated
PLUS: *SHOWN* appreciation by receiver

← Worth It   Calculation is constantly happening   NOT Worth It →

The RESULT is the goal being evaluated. It can take the shape of an outcome, an impact produced, an upside created, a difference made, something provided, or a problem solved.

The hunter will subtract the resources required to meet the goal from the initial value assigned to the goal. The resources we have to spend are Money, Energy, and Time. I list them in this order to create the acronym "MET," as in how the goal will be met.

Next, the hunter will subtract the sacrifice required or anticipated to meet the goal, understanding that resources spent on this goal can't be spent on anything else. A simple example is if the goal is to paint a room, the money, energy, and time spent to accomplish this task will not be available for a family vacation.

Then, the hunter will add to the equation the value of SHOWN appreciation. **Appreciation that is not expressed has no impact.** However, **sincere appreciation expressed to another person**, especially to a hunter who is constantly calculating how they are expending their money, energy, and time, **is like adding bonus points to the value of the result**. Think of it as dividends on an investment. The costs are less impactful because the benefit is greater.

This process is a calculation, NOT an equation—because the value of the result is constantly changing as situations change. If you have ever done a remodeling project, you are very familiar with how something that seemed Worth-It at the start can relatively quickly become not Worth-It if the costs become too high. The point is that someone in Hunting Mode is keenly aware they will "die" if they don't get back more than they put in. Oh, there it is again—the instinct to survive!

For both males and females in Hunting Mode, this calculation is constantly occurring. Particularly for men, it happens at an instinctual level in the background and sometimes consciously in the foreground.

An easy way to see the Worth-It Calculation at work is as hunters and gatherers approach the remote control for the television. I'll use my husband and me as an example. When my husband uses the remote control, he quickly changes the channels or scrolls through the channel guide, rapidly and repeatedly calculating that a show is "NOT WORTH-IT." Meanwhile, I sit there in gathering mode, becoming anxious because we haven't checked out all the details of each show. I reason that we may be missing something we need now or maybe later. Is it any wonder there is friction and fights over the remote control when individuals are unaware of what is driving the other person's actions? Once again, neither person is misbehaving, but both are misunderstanding.

Let's delve a little more into the value of the RESULT using a scale of 1-10, with number one being NOT WORTH-IT and number ten being WORTH-IT!!!

Hopefully, the chart below will help convey the wide spectrum of the RESULT VALUE.

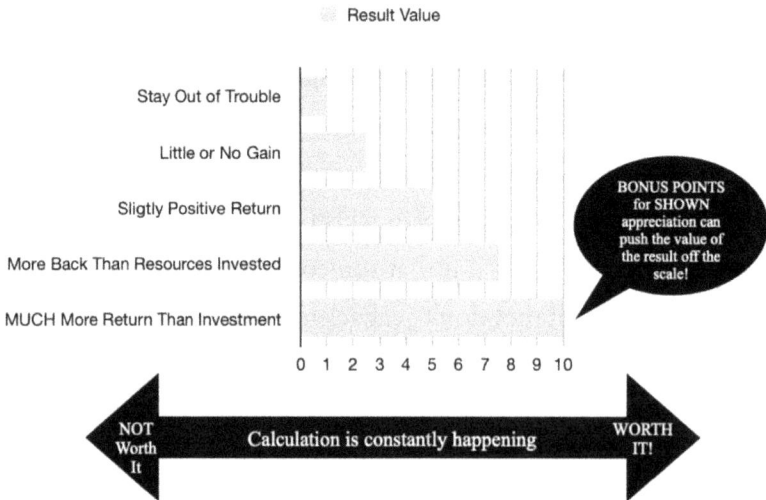

Are you curious why "Stay Out of Trouble" is listed as a category for results? The answer is simple: Staying out of trouble is a huge motivation for estrogen-based individuals. Historically, safety was key for survival—that's a great motivator for something to be Worth-It, correct? As we've discovered, having connection led to safety, so acting in ways that kept our tribe from being upset or displeased with us became very Worth-It! Think again about how you feel when your texts go unanswered. This is the same instinct still at work in our lives today.

Problems occur when women project onto men that staying out of trouble is a motivator for making something Worth-It. There are a couple of ways this shows up in our interactions.

First, women tend to intentionally withhold appreciation (rather than show it), believing this will make a man try harder to earn her appreciation. That is, after all, how she, as a woman, would respond to withheld appreciation.

Second, women express how upset they are to men, thinking this will motivate a man. NEWS FLASH: A caveman was not the least bit concerned if the large beast he was hunting or the marauders attacking his tribe were upset with him! Staying out of trouble does not even register on a man's Worth-It Calculation.

So, what motivates male hunters when interacting with women and makes a goal Worth-It? As the graph indicates, making progress towards a specific result, with added "BONUS POINTS" for sincerely shown appreciation. Expressed appreciation tells a man he has also *produced a second significant result*—an enhanced quality of life for a woman he cares for, whom he has made happy.

Did you catch that? The reason men want to protect and provide for women is NOT because they think we are incompetent, incapable, or stupid. Most men, most of the time, think women are amazing. Men may not be aware of Hunting and Gathering Modes, but they still appreciate women's ability to switch between them quickly. Part of a man's admiration is expressed by his desire to enhance a woman's life!! A woman's sincerely shown appreciation tells him he is succeeding.

Ladies, please take some time to let this new information saturate your viewpoint. This perspective can be challenging to digest as it is the opposite of what society currently teaches. Countless times in the past, I declined the unsolicited help a man offered me. My viewpoint was that he was insulting me. What a wonderful world it is when we allow ourselves to see and receive all the help surrounding us. I've tested out receiving help from my husband, work colleagues, and men in grocery stores whom I don't know, all while generously expressing my appreciation. It's consistently been a win/win for all involved!

The absolute bull's eye of Worth-It motivation for men is to make a woman's dream come true.

In 2018, that is exactly what my husband did for me.

Shortly after I began my studies for my licensing and certification in this material, it became apparent that it would take about thirty hours a week for me to achieve my dream. This was in addition to my full-time job of forty-five hours a week. My instincts loudly told me my husband couldn't be happy with me about this. Danger! Danger!

I remember sharing my concerns with him. Before he had time to respond, I added that I was sure I could somehow figure out a way to do everything I needed to do, plus have time to get away with him. He looked truly baffled that I was so worried.

His response dumbfounded me. He said he had already assumed he wouldn't see me much during that year, but he knew becoming licensed and certified would be a dream come true for me. The time my dream would require wasn't a problem for him. He'd already told his friends he would have extra time to spend with them because I would be busy all year. He told me, "It's OK—because you want to do this, and I support you."

Can you see how he had already worked through his Worth-It Calculation? He knew the goal, had factored in all the costs, including sacrifices, and had concluded that the value of the result was WORTH-IT to him to make me happy. I have to tell you, he is my hero!

But the story doesn't end there. Because I knew my husband would not say something just to stay out of trouble, I accepted and believed what he told me. When I shared the irony with him, he replied, "I'm glad you can understand. I wouldn't have said it if it wasn't true."

Essential #5 - Listening to Learn

Listening to Learn is the fifth essential for better responses, results, and relationships. It requires exercising an intangible quality out of your Human Spirit. You need curiosity to listen for three things that I call a person's MIC.

- What *Matters* to a person.
- What's *Important* to a person.
- What a person *Cares* about.

Listening to Learn requires shifting our listening point of view. Instead of concentrating on what we want or need, we become intentionally aware of what the person in front of us is saying about who they are. This choice overrides the default listening styles of both Hunting and Gathering Modes.

Listening to Learn creates an opportunity to discover a person's Dearest Goals and Heart's Desires (something we will examine more deeply in Chapter 9). Talk about creating connection!

While listening to hunters, one caveat to remember is that they instinctively conceal their strengths and weaknesses in order not to compromise their ability to produce a result. For a hunter—whether male or female—to reveal their MIC to you, one of two things must be in place. The hunter must know from experience that the listener will not hurt them with what they share, or the hunter must know that the listener cannot hurt them because they will likely never see them again. I've had that second scenario happen many times on planes.

To successfully Listen to Learn, you will need two tools. First, imaginary duct tape. Second, the awareness that men speak literally.

Let's delve a little deeper into imaginary duct tape.

Do you remember that I shared that most men, most of the time, are in Hunting Mode, which makes them single-focused and committed? Because of that mindset, when a man is asked a question, he is committed to the answer he provides. Therefore, it may take up to thirty seconds for him to respond. To allow the time he needs to commit to his answer, ask one question only. Then, apply your imaginary duct tape and wait thirty seconds. Do not interrupt him by rephrasing your question or providing more details.

When I first started doing this, I literally counted the seconds in my head. Trust me, thirty seconds can seem like an eternity. If the man pauses as he answers, repeat this process by asking him, "Anything else?" Then, reapply the imagery duct tape. Keep repeating this sequence. You don't have to worry about knowing when he is finished. Eventually, when you ask, "Anything else?" he will say something along the lines of, "No, that's all," or "I can't think of anything."

To illustrate how literal men are, imagine a husband and wife sitting on their couch. The wife asks her husband, "Hon, where do you *want* to go for our vacation this year?"

He starts to think about his answer. He doesn't want to give an answer that he cannot keep. Possible thoughts going through his mind would be, *Oh, I've always wanted to go to Hawaii. Walking next to her on a beautiful beach …hmmm, but would we be able to do that on our budget?* Meanwhile, he has not said anything.

Because he has not said anything, she begins thinking, *He must not have understood my question. I'll rephrase it.* So she says, "Hon, where do you *think we should* go for our vacation?"

She has just interrupted his attempt to give her a committed answer.

Now his thoughts go to something like, *Wait. Does she want to know where I WANT to go or where WE SHOULD go? I want to go to Hawaii, but we probably SHOULD go see her mother.* Again, he has still not said anything.

By this time, the woman is convinced she must have married an idiot. She decides to make it easy for him and give him multiple choices, and says something like, "Hon, do you want to go to Florida or California for our vacation?" She interrupted his attempt to provide a committed answer for the second time.

In frustration, he snaps at her. "You obviously don't care what I THINK, so just go wherever you want!"

She feels hurt and crushed and thinks, *He doesn't want to spend any time with me!*

There was no misbehaving by either of them. But there certainly was a lot of misunderstanding.

Listening to Learn was literally a life-changer for me. On my four-hour drive home from the first class that exposed me to this information, I was beyond skeptical that what I'd learned would work in real life. Instead, I tried to figure out how to teach everything I'd learned to my husband.

When I walked in the door, without thinking, I asked my husband, "What filled your weekend?" Almost simultaneously, I thought, *Ughhh, that's my one question!* I immediately chose to put on my imaginary duct tape and wait. I was pretty shocked that at twenty-five seconds, he started to talk.

I followed the instructions I'd received to simply ask, "Anything else?" when he paused.

He talked for about twenty minutes and then told me, "I think that's everything." I was just about to ask a second question when he said, "Oh, but that was only Friday night, on Saturday night ..." Then, he talked for another twenty minutes to provide a complete answer to my question.

I could hear tumblers clicking into place as my husband behaved exactly as I was taught men behave. Revelation quickly dawned that I had been interrupting my husband for thirty-seven years. Yikes! No wonder he was frustrated and short with me much of the time. Sudden clarity filled me. I didn't need to teach my husband everything I'd learned. Rather, I needed to use the tools I had learned to grow and begin seeing him for who he truly is.

Essential #6 - Look for Clark Kent

No joke, there are "superheroes" all around us. But, sometimes the lens we use to see the world prevents us from seeing them. The information in this book provides opportunities for you to choose a new lens. Having an open mind to try out new lenses is how you look for the "Clark Kents" in your life each day. This is the sixth foundational essential we can use to experience better results, responses, and relationships. Together, we will continue to build our capacity to do this through the remaining eight chapters.

My friend Melissa shared her real-life experience of finding her Clark Kent.

Melissa has a son, John, who is in his early thirties. In the past, she had viewed John as too busy, focused, and preoccupied with his schedule to make it possible for her to ask him to help her care for her dad—his granddad. Melissa was pretty sure that if she asked John for his help, he would be reluctant and inconvenienced.

When Melissa shared her story with me, she had already completed my series of topics. Some of the specific "aha's" she experienced were that men are naturally wired to provide, solve problems, meet the needs of the people they care about, and, last but not least, be heroes. Melissa also learned how important it is to speak directly to the point or to the problem. She'd consciously been trying to put these revelations into practice.

A situation arose where Melissa had to go out of town. While she was gone, she received a call that her dad needed help. Her initial response was, "What am I going to do?" Then, it dawned on her that John might respond positively if he knew he was saving the day by helping. John might solve her problem! Remembering these facts armed Melissa with the courage to ask John for his help.

She called her son and was very specific in asking him what she needed. She told John what it would provide for her—peace of mind. Melissa was surprised by John's response. It was filled with obvious delight and a wholehearted willingness to help her. A beautiful opportunity was created to tell her son, "You are my hero!"

Melissa told me, "I could almost see John taking off his 'Clark Kent glasses,' donning his superhero cape, and rushing to 'save' me, his mom, from worry."

Melissa's deeper understanding of the differences between men and women, mixed with a willingness to see her son in a new light, set up a win/win for both of them.

Who is your Clark Kent?

Chapter 1 - Questions

1. What three questions help us see one another with more understanding?

2. What points of view do you have that are helpful to you? Unhelpful?

3. What is the biggest problem when we live solely out of our instincts? What other capacities do we have within us to resolve that problem?

4. What have been your personal experiences with Hunting Mode and Gathering Mode?

5. Explain the Worth-It Calculation in your own words. Give an example where you have seen it in your experiences.

6. What intangible quality and tool are required when practicing Listening to Learn?

REALITY CHECK:

- Look for Hunting and Gathering Modes in yourself and those around you.

- Ladies, practice either *asking* a man for help or *accepting* unsolicited offers of help. Then, receive that help with genuine, shown appreciation. Watch how he responds. (This could be as simple as asking a man in a grocery store to reach an item off a high shelf.)

Chapter Two

Six Stumbling Blocks Uncovered

"It's obvious."

Has that ever been your assumption when interacting with others? We make statements, send emails, shoot off texts, and think that what we communicate is "obvious" and how the recipient should respond is "obvious."

I know I've done it many times. The problem is, the only person who thinks what I'm communicating is obvious is me. Hmmm ... could that create problems?

Remember our avocado and lime from Chapter 1? This chapter provides an opportunity to look for and intentionally interact with differences between genders. By doing this, we gain the capacity for better connections.

The intangible quality prevalent in this chapter is understanding.

We are building an awareness of five facets of male etiquette: team, competition, loyalty, privacy, and honor.

For both men and women, responses to a breach of etiquette happen in the Human Raw component of our being. Because these responses occur at an instinctual level, they are quicker than cognitive thought. Whether you are male or female, our Human Raw component believes that breaches of etiquette happen for one of two reasons: The person committing the breach is doing this on purpose, or they are too stupid to care or know proper etiquette and are, therefore, not worth cluing in.

Ladies, the breaches of male etiquette discussed in this chapter are as repulsive to men as burping or farting at the dinner table are to women. No joke.

This chapter aims to create awareness of these Human Raw breaches. Then, we will add in the qualities of our soul (will, intellect, and emotion) and mix that with the intangible qualities of understanding and compassion. If this sounds familiar, it should. It is the process you will see over and over again to create better responses, results, and relationships. It's how we move from our Human Raw component to our Human Spirit. The result is experiencing living from partnership and abundance rather than scarcity.

A quick reminder: you may encounter some resistance to the material in this chapter. Should this happen, I encourage you to review the three points of view discussed in Chapter 1. This will hopefully help you identify what's causing your resistance.

Stumbling Block #1 - "It's obvious."

I'll be the first to admit—the question "What's wrong with you?" has crossed my mind many times when I've gotten a response I was not expecting. It can feel like I've hit something, but I have no idea what, much like what happens when we are driving and hit something we don't see because it was in our blind spot.

I know I'm not the only driver who has encountered blind spots since many car manufacturers now include blind spot indicators. The first time I drove a rental car with this feature, I thought, *This is great.* If you feel similarly, you will greatly appreciate the data in this chapter, because it empowers you to see the blind spots between genders. Understanding and choosing to use this information can prevent much wear and tear on everyone involved.

Before we go any further, let's look at the definition of "etiquette" so we are all on the same page. Etiquette is the customary code of polite behavior in society or among members of a particular profession or group.

When etiquette is breached, not just the forms reviewed in this chapter, the Human Raw response for either gender is to judge the offender as a crass outsider who doesn't belong or fit in. To the person whose etiquette has been breached—"it's obvious."

Our response to a breach may range from putting up with it to, if we deem the behavior completely unacceptable, ostracizing the offender. Sadly, since "it's obvious" to the person whose etiquette was breached, there is a very good chance the one who violated the etiquette won't receive an explanation but simply be cut off by the offended person or group.

Now, imagine yourself at your local big-box store, standing in front of a wall of different light bulbs. Everything on that wall is a light bulb, but there are many unique types, right? Every one of these bulbs is wired differently. If you don't understand how a bulb is wired and attempt to connect it incorrectly, it will not provide light. However, when each bulb's unique wiring is respected and used appropriately—voilà, success!

This chapter is about male and female wiring rather than our different operating modes. The point is that our respective wiring is not right or wrong. It is not good or bad. We are simply wired differently. We want to harness those differences and put them to good use.

This information will shed light on the times you have not understood the responses of or have been misunderstood by the opposite gender.

Stumbling Block #2 - Team Etiquette

The first thing I discovered while conducting my research about male etiquette and teams is that genders have different definitions for "team." Below is a summary list comparing the different etiquettes of male and female teams. Under the chart, I will provide more details for each of the six points.

Male Etiquette	Female Etiquette
A team is a group with a united purpose or goal.	A team is a group where everyone has equal status.
Who is going to lead?	Who are YOU to lead?
What's the plan?	Questions the plan.
What's my part?	I'll do that for you.
To move forward—Is my part meaningful?	To move forward—Everyone must agree.
Part of male DNA—Literally.	Not part of DNA.

Without any additional explanation, can you see from this chart how easily breaches of etiquette and misunderstandings can occur without more awareness and understanding? Please remember that the above table refers to most men and most women most of the time. There will be exceptions.

Let's start with the definition of a team. For males, the most important facet of a team is having a united purpose or goal. For females, the most important facet is that everyone on the team has equal status.

Before you roll your eyes, understand that at an instinctual level, females confuse "equality" with "status." Unlike males, viewing different roles/parts as equally important is difficult for females. The reason is that for much of history, it was ingrained in women that their safety, and therefore survival, was dependent on their status in their tribe, which was determined by their role. Whereas for males, the importance and value of different roles were evident when they went on a hunt or into battle. This mindset leads us to the next point.

Males automatically look for and recognize leadership. The ever-present Worth-It Calculation makes males aware that leadership causes a team to pull together and make the best use of their resources.

Conversely, when a woman sees someone step up to lead in a team situation, their instincts unconsciously trigger the reaction, "Who are YOU to lead?" Females perceive a difference in roles as a threat. Female instincts scream at us, creating tension and intensely reminding us that everyone needs to be equal for "me" to be safe. Are you noticing how prevalent safety is to a female's thoughts? At the root of every decision as a female is an instinctual question, "Am I safe?"

Moving on with the etiquette of male teams, immediately after recognizing a leader, males look for The Plan. What plan? THE PLAN they believe provides the best possibility for them to achieve the goal successfully. At an instinctual level for males, The Plan carries a weight of life and death importance because it is integral to producing a result. One of the facets of males spending most of their time in Hunting Mode is an unconscious awareness that an individual and a tribe cannot survive without producing results. Chapter 5 provides a much more in-depth study of The Plan.

Contrarily, because of the diffuse awareness, which is part of Gathering Mode, females question The Plan. They will ask questions like, "Have you thought of this detail, person, or possibility?" Generally, women are completely unaware of the large breach of etiquette they have just committed by questioning The Plan that males believe will guarantee success.

With a leader and plan in place, males look for the answer to, "What is my part?" This is easy to see on sports teams—am I the running back, quarterback, or defensive lineman?

In contrast, females figure out the responsibilities of other team members and think they are helping when they say, "I'll do that for you." This action is spurred by a female's instincts, which tell her that a person will like and protect her more if she does their part for them. This is a HUGE breach of male etiquette!!

Men experience a woman offering to do their part as disrespect. A man does not understand why she wouldn't let him do HIS part. When I discussed this with a mid-sixties man on my research panel, he told me, "That's a real hot button for me. Not many things get me going, but that does."

His response made me curious, so I asked him if other men think this way.

He said, "Yeah. I think it's a pretty common thing. I've heard, 'Do YOU wanna fly this plane?' 'Do you think YOU can do a better job than this?'" He explained that the point of these statements is to "put people in their place."

Have you ever heard the expression, "She doesn't know her place?" Did that make the hair on the back of your neck stand up, ladies?? I have good news. It is not the personal demeaning slam women perceive it to be. Males understand the unstated end of that sentence is "ON THE TEAM." The concern is when a woman—or anyone—overreaches their part/role on the team, that overreach disrespects another person's ability to perform their role. The Hunting Mode's instinctual response is danger, danger! The success of The Plan is being threatened. *If you are doing my part, who is doing your part? Are we vulnerable?* This instinct goes all the way back to everyone in the tribe knowing their part in The Plan for the tribe to survive.

It's time to share an embarrassing moment. While writing this book, I unintentionally experienced the intensity of disrespecting my husband by overreaching. We were in the car together when the topic of where he would be working that weekend came up. I immediately pulled out my phone to look up gas prices in that part of town. I knew they would be cheaper. My instincts were at work, telling me that looking up and sharing this information would be helpful and make him happy. Quite the opposite! He raised his voice and said, "Do you think I'm an idiot??"

I was crushed that my "help" had been rejected. I was angry at his raised voice. We were still close to our home, and without thinking, I said, "Please pull into that parking lot, and I will walk home. You obviously don't want to be with me right now." He was stunned at my response. There was no conversation for a few moments. He took the initiative to try and thoughtfully explain to me that all he was doing was sharing the facts of his experience resulting from my actions.

We each chose to believe the best of the other person and continued on our way. However, there was still tension between us.

After dinner, he asked me if I had enjoyed our afternoon together.

I responded, "I did enjoy our dinner. I did not enjoy fighting."

He looked at me with surprise and said, "I didn't think we were fighting."

You could have knocked me over with a feather. Did he seriously think that? He shared again that he was simply stating the facts of his experience. I was sure I was somehow misunderstanding him, but in that moment, I couldn't figure out how.

A few days later, as I edited this section of the book, there was the answer right in front of me! I had disrespected him by trying to do his part. I am thankful to those who equipped me with the ability to understand what had transpired. I was able to completely let go and no longer carry the hurt and anger that would have festered otherwise.

The next natural step for male team etiquette is to apply the Worth-It Calculation to determine if their part is meaningful. If their part does not pass this test, males won't move forward by being on the team.

Whereas for women to be able to move forward with a team, everyone must agree.

All of these facets of male team etiquette are driven by the fact that TEAM is literally in men's DNA. Tests conducted with sperm in Petri dishes have demonstrated that even at this cellular level, three teams are formed: blockers, killers, and runners. All have one common goal of procreation. Females do not have this in their DNA.

Comparing this list of attributes for male and female team etiquette, can you see how easily we breach one another's etiquette when it comes to teams? Again, it's not because anyone is misbehaving; the breaches come from misunderstanding.

During my research, one male panel member in his late twenties shared both his frustrations and his appreciation of male/female differences. I asked him, "What was it like for you working on a team with more females than males?"

He answered, "It was me trying to reel them in to have a specific goal/mission for the team."

I put on my imaginary duct tape and waited to see if he had anything else to say.

He continued, "Women think of the extra factors. They typically find the things that aren't on the list but are actually needed, too."

This is an excellent example of mixing awareness and understanding to create a win/win result for everyone.

Both male and female etiquette teams are clearly able to reach a goal—they just arrive there very differently. Male etiquette is a pretty straight line composed of the following:

- What's the goal?
- Who's the leader?
- What's The Plan?
- Is my part meaningful
- Let's do this!

Female etiquette looks more like a large, starry vortex that, as it spins, pulls in as many options as possible as it circles toward the goal.

Kristin was a thirty-year-old woman who participated in my research on this topic. She shared her experience of different team etiquette with me.

Kristin grew up in male-team-etiquette sports. She competed quite a bit and currently works in a male-dominated office. Her exposure to female teams is with a team of women volunteering at her church.

As we discussed the different dynamics of male and female teams, the light bulb went on for Kristin. She shared with me that she had been pretty frustrated with the team of women at her church. Suddenly, she understood why decisions and actions happen so quickly at her job, where she is the only woman in an office full of men. It also made much more sense to her why it requires so much additional time to move forward with the team of women with whom she volunteers. Kristin said, "While I enjoy the relationships, it has been an adjustment making time for things to happen with the team of women."

Are you able to see how having this information and harnessing the two different points of view could be helpful not only in your personal relationships but also in your work environments?

Stumbling Block #3 - Loyalty Etiquette

Can you relate to this scene? A man and woman are in a car. The man is driving. Suddenly, another vehicle cuts in front of them. The man starts to shout at the driver who cut them off. The woman definitely feels unsafe because they were cut off; however, the man's frustration and anger seem like a bigger threat to her safety because he is immediately next to her in the close confines of the vehicle, and she can't get away from him. Her female instincts compel her to try to "calm this tiger next to her" so she will be safe.

She tries to diffuse the incident by making excuses for the unknown driver. Her comment would be something along the lines of, "They're probably just having a bad day and didn't mean to do that." Not only does this not calm the man, but it also increases his anger and frustration. Why? At an instinctual level, the man perceives the woman's actions as being complete-ly DISLOYAL. From the man's perspective, the woman has taken the side of the unknown stranger who is a threat to them both. If she were being loyal, she would appreciate him for keeping them safe and agree with him that the other driver acted poorly.

I have been that "disloyal woman" many times in the past without having any clue how I had breached male loyalty etiquette. Now, when a situation like this occurs, I immediately get on my husband's team, agreeing with his evaluation of the other driver. If my husband is yelling, "What a jerk!" my response is, "Yeah, that driver is definitely a jerk!" The stress level in our car quickly evaporates, and we continue to enjoy our ride together. Who knew? Not me, but I am thankful I know now.

As I dug deeper into my research to uncover more specifics about male loyalty etiquette, I asked multiple men, "How do you define loyalty?"

A man in his mid-fifties answered,
"Loyalty doesn't cut and run at the first sign
of disagreement or discord."

A man in his mid-thirties responded,
"Loyalty is people committed to me being my best me
even on my bad days."

Can you see how these quotes incorporate the attributes of male loyalty etiquette outlined below?

- Males are loyal to those who ARE giving them something they need. Some examples of those things would be friendship, leader-ship, teammates, and family.

- Once males have decided to be loyal:

  ○ They will be loyal through thick and thin.

  ○ They will have the other person's back, whether or not they agree with that person.

  ○ They consider selling someone out for being wrong as unthinkable.

You may have seen male loyalty in real life or in a movie where two men are in a bar. One of those two men hears a comment by a third person that really upsets him to the point that he begins a fight. His buddy is right there with him, taking and giving punches, even if he thinks his friend is an idiot for starting this fight. It won't be until later, when they are alone together, that the buddy who stood up for his friend will say something like, "What were you thinking?"

Let's compare the above attributes to female loyalty etiquette. However, before we do that, please remember that the female attributes below all occur at the instinctual Human Raw level, which means quicker than cognitive thought. Females can absolutely choose from their Human Spirit to act similarly to male loyalty, but it's not "built-in" and, therefore, requires much more effort.

Attributes of female loyalty etiquette are:

- A female will be loyal to those she THINKS she needs on her side to keep her safe.

  ○ If she thinks a person is bigger and stronger, she will be safe. So she will be loyal.

  ○ If she thinks you're correct, she will be safe. So she will be loyal.

- ○ If she thinks you're not stupid, she will be safe. So she will be loyal

- For females, getting past their instinctual responses and being loyal at all costs is a huge act of Human Spirit.

Most females don't even see how conditional their loyalty is because the need to feel safe is such a strong instinctual drive. The tension from their instincts makes their choices *obvious* to them. They believe their choices just make sense.

A woman in her early fifties described receiving this type of conditional loyalty this way: "I didn't know that some people would measure loyalty by agreement instead of respect. It was disappointing and hurtful."

When I asked a man in his mid-fifties what he experiences if someone is only loyal when they agree with you, he answered, "To me, that is not really loyalty."

Can we agree that what we all genuinely want when it comes to loyalty is a true friend who will always have our back?

But what does it mean to males for someone to have your back? The expression comes from a time when battles were fought with hand-to-hand combat. Two warriors literally stood back-to-back. Together, they had a 360-degree view of the threats coming at them.

While conducting my research, I asked a man in his mid-sixties what it meant for someone to have his back. He said, "Somebody that I can rely on and that is going to be a support and advocate for me and not ever a detractor or underminer."

I asked a man in his mid-thirties how he would handle someone in his "loyal circle" doing something wrong or stupid. His response was, "I try to be in closer communication than I typically would in order to let them know 1) that I am there for them and 2) not to let life break the relationship."

The depth of commitment in these answers made me curious. I asked multiple men, "What's possible when you know someone has your back?" Here are some responses I received:

"It gives you the ability to be completely transparent."
–mid-sixties male

"Failure. I don't have to hide. I can be my authentic self."
–mid-thirties male

"It makes me feel I could be an agent for change."
–mid-twenties male

I want to live in a world where people can be this transparent, authentic, and courageous. How about you?

I *repeat*, females can choose to be loyal at all costs. However, choosing requires holding space in their thoughts, words, and deeds so they can move past their instincts. Plus, they must mix in the intangible qualities of understanding and faithfulness. Men, I suggest being aware of and looking for when a woman is acting this way. Don't miss the opportunity to express appreciation for her choice and action, recognizing that this is not part of how she is wired at her Human Raw level.

Not too long after learning about what it means to have a person's back, I had a real-life experience of it at my job. I was planning a function for 120 people and found out three weeks before the event that I needed to have unexpected surgery four days before the start of the event. My boss was traveling, so I notified him via email. My last sentence was, "Sorry to add one more problem to your plate."

My instincts caused me tremendous tension, telling me I was no longer the strongest horse and would be abandoned. I was totally undone by my boss's response: "Not a problem, Diane. We will figure it out. Main thing is that you get healthy. We'll talk about a game plan when I get back in on Tuesday."

I sat there and let his reply soak in. I could literally see that my boss had my back. I was able to receive his genuine gift of loyalty. He was true to his word about solving the problem. He and another vice president sought my advice to find out what help we needed. Then, they took care of providing it.

Stumbling Block #4 - Competition Etiquette

Yes, I'm repeating myself, but before exploring male and female competition etiquette, please remember we are talking about differences in male and female wiring and the instinctual responses—which occur before cognitive thought. One caveat I would provide for this particular stumbling block is that young women are becoming immersed in competitive sports at younger ages, which is helping women develop their competitive drive. These are cognitive skills. This doesn't mean the instinctual responses we will discuss below are not still present under the surface.

Let's look at both the male and female viewpoints of competition etiquette with quotes to expand each point.

MALE VIEWPOINT

- **Competition is a way to put best beside best to grow and improve.**

  I asked a mid-twenties male research participant how early males start putting best beside best. He answered by telling me about his sons, who are two and three years old. "My two sons are constantly competing with each other. I don't think I taught them that. I think they just are that way."

- **Competition is fun!**

  I asked a mid-sixties male research participant what is fun about competition. He replied, "You are trying to be better; that's the benefit and the real reason for competition. I think it's fun in that if you achieve that [being better], you win either way. Even if you don't win that particular contest, you are a better person for trying."

- **Competition strengthens a team.**

  A man in his early 50s shared with me how competition strengthens the work team he manages. He told me, "Somebody who is competitive can push somebody less competitive to achieve things they would not have done otherwise."

- **Competition creates gratitude.**

  I asked a mid-30s male research participant, "Have you ever experienced gratitude/appreciation for a competitor?" He said: "Of course I have! How could I not appreciate what he's accomplished, even if I didn't enjoy that he was better than me?"

- **Competition comes from a place of honor.**
  I asked my husband, "Do you think about honor and competition very much?" He responded, "I think about both pretty much constantly. If you win the competition without being honorable, it's a pretty hollow win."

FEMALE VIEWPOINT

The explanation below each point is a compilation of replies from multiple women.

- **Competition is childish and immature.**
  You should just get over it and grow up.

- **Competition creates anger.**
  The survival instinct, driven by the need to be connected to be safe, is totally at odds with competition and tells women they simply can't win. Female instincts send one of two messages: If you win, this person will disconnect from you because you beat them. If you lose, this person will disconnect from you because you are not worth being around. Not surprisingly, this makes women angry.

- **Competition can destroy relationships.**
  This is the fruit of the point immediately above. Believing there is no way to win, females conclude that competition can actually destroy relationships.

- **Competition creates angst and upset.**
  Angst and upset are a result of female instincts screaming, "Why can't we all just get along and stay connected? Why do we have to compete?"

- **Competition can sometimes escalate to feelings of hatred.**
  As all of the above instinctual tension grows in females, it can sometimes reach the point of hatred because women start to see those who compete with them as the enemy.

It's pretty clear that at our Human Raw level, the male and female points of view about competition are close to polar opposites. A minefield of misunderstandings can happen when choices are not made from the Human Spirit's awareness and understanding of these differences.

Ladies, I hope learning how men use competition as a tool to grow and improve themselves will help you embrace our competition etiquette differences. The saying below, that many attribute to Nelson Mandela, really summed up the positive power of competition for me.

"I never lose. I either win or learn."
–Nelson Mandela

Stumbling Block #5 - Privacy Etiquette

This stumbling block refers to privacy and how we interact with information (not about alone-time privacy). By now, I don't think you will be surprised to find out that there are significant differences in male and female etiquette wiring when it comes to how we approach sharing information.

For this topic, I asked all the men on my research panel, "What does it mean when someone says, 'This is between you and me.'" Three points were consistent throughout their answers.

The first common theme was that multiple men used the expression "holding a confidence." One man described this as "The door is shut. No more sharing." Can you hear the guardianship expressed in his answer?

The second theme was the "Man Rule." A man in his early fifties provided wonderful insight into this: "Don't talk about how a man has failed because that goes to the meat of a man's soul. Just don't do that!" When a man has trusted you with this type of information, it shouldn't go any further.

The third theme was the "Code of Honor," which is all about respect. This particular point of male etiquette can cause misunderstandings and hurt feelings when women are unaware of it. When a woman encounters a man who is living the Code of Honor, she will notice that he does not ask the woman many questions to learn about her. The woman's instinctual interpretation is thoughts such as: *He's not interested in me. He's closed off.* Or, *He won't connect.* Can you relate, ladies?

In actuality, the man is showing deep respect for the woman! Remember, hunters instinctively do not share strengths and weaknesses in an effort to avoid compromising achieving a result. Therefore, *not* asking another to share such information is an expression of respect and honor. The male perspective is: *If you want me to know something about you, you will tell me.*

If you are a woman reading this, there's a good chance you are starting to feel agitated and wondering, *Following this logic, how is it even possible to have a conversation?* Actually, it's simpler than you can imagine.

To be respectful, rather than prying, ask men your questions in this format: "Is there anything you would like me to know about..."—finish the question with something like "...your day?" "...your plan?" or "...your golf game?" This question sends the man on a hunt for what he does want you to know. He can easily manage what information he is comfortable sharing. A quick reminder to apply your imaginary duct tape after asking this question.

In reverse, if a woman wants a man to know more about her, she can start the conversation with this question: "May I tell you about something that really interests me/I care about/am passionate about?" My experience is that men truly enjoy hearing a woman share with them about any of these things. There is only one forewarning you need to know. Men will be very honest about whether they have the time to listen to you at that moment. Their answer could range from "I'd love to hear that" to "I don't have much time right now, but I'd love to hear about this. Could we have this conversation_____?" Choosing to be aware of this can prevent women from instinctively thinking, *He's blowing me off.*

In a strictly business situation, a respectful way to ask to share information is to say, "May I tell you about something I think would help us be really successful?"

Misunderstandings erupt when females project onto males their perspective of the importance of sharing information driven by their instinct to connect. At the Human Raw level, female instincts exert pressure to share insider information to create the status and connection she believes she needs to be safe. However, by acting in this manner, a woman portrays to a man that she is not someone he can trust. She creates a breach that prevents the connection she is seeking to establish. Similarly, females share private information with other females to be included, connected, and safe. It is a victory of Human Spirit for women not to share private information or to first ask permission to share.

Learning this was very helpful to me during the time I helped care for my father-in-love in his final years. Not only did he share very private information with me, but he also authorized his medical doctors to share information with me. When I became aware of something I thought my husband needed to know, I would first ask my father-in-love for permission to share specific information with my husband. If he approved, I would start the conversation with my husband by saying, "Your dad gave me his permission to tell you ..." This created trust and respect between my father-in-love and me, as well as between my husband and me.

Stumbling Block #6 - Honor Etiquette

Before examining how male honor etiquette is breached, we must first understand how men characterize honor.

When I asked the men on my research panel to define honor, the unanimous answer was some expression of being true to yourself. This collective response was even more impactful because it came from men aged seventeen to sixty-five, with representation from each decade in between.

I learned that for most men, most of the time, honor is what directs their choices and, therefore, their path.

The following two quotes delineate how much honor plays a part in how men live.

"If you can be true to yourself and
don't let anyone persuade you
out of being what you know is the thing to do,
to me, that's honor."
–mid-sixties male research panel member

"Honor is knowing my true north;
knowing what is it most like me to be,
and be that."
–mid-fifties male research panel member

Learning what honor meant to men piqued my curiosity to ask the man who provided the second quote above, "What is it to honor another man?" He told me, "Honor is when you celebrate a guy for his successes, and you don't beat him to death for his failure."

Are you wondering how men live out honoring one another? I did, too. I discovered this is accomplished by men making space for another man's strengths and expertise. One male research panel member shared a beautiful example when he described a "man trip"—yes, that is how he literally described a fishing trip. The men honored one another by swapping roles regularly throughout the day, depending on who had the expertise for the moment. To attain the desired result, the goal, combined with each man's particular skill set, determined who was most qualified to lead the group.

Can you see how expressing honor ties back to men putting importance on knowing their part on a team? The respect and value men place on each person's role becomes a vehicle to honor one another. This is the opposite of females not being comfortable or not feeling safe when these distinctions are made on a team.

You now have a deeper insight into the male etiquette breach that occurs when women over-reach by trying to do a male team member's part for them. The man you just tried to help has been both dishonored and disrespected.

As I was concluding my research on honor, I asked my husband, "Does honor trump loyalty?" He told me:

"Being true to yourself trumps everything, doesn't it?"

This quote summed up everything about male etiquette. It's not hard for me to choose to act out of Human Spirit and get behind the male etiquette perspective of team, competition, loyalty, and privacy when I understand that behind all of it is honor and being true to yourself. How about you?

I personally discovered that I have unwittingly breached male honor etiquette with my husband.

Many times in the past, I have been frustrated when my husband has chosen to fulfill a commitment with disregard for his health. Here is one example.

My husband is the president of our homeowner's association. Our neighborhood was in the midst of opposing a new development immediately across from our subdivision; one particular evening, my husband was not feeling well and was stressed from the demands on his time. I suggested to him that maybe if he took care of his health first, it would be easier to fight this fight.

He told me very firmly, "I know you disagree with the order I'm doing things, but this is the way it's going to be."

I really struggled not to blow up at him out of the fear I was feeling about his health. The only words I could get out at that moment were, "Go. Just go."

He did. He went to his office without saying another word. We didn't speak again that evening.

I was angry, confused, hurt, and scared. I remember thinking, *What just happened??? All my training to understand our differences and conversations like this still happen?*

Suddenly, I remembered my husband's quote: "Being true to yourself trumps everything, doesn't it?" I slapped myself on the forehead, realizing he was doing exactly that!! He was being true to himself. He had made a commitment to lead our HOA. In his words, "to be the watchdog for our community and to bark at anyone who tries to enter."

As I replayed our conversation, I could see how quickly my instinct had kicked in, telling me, "Danger! Danger! If he doesn't take care of himself first, he won't be around to take care of me." My fear made it feel like he was being disloyal to me, even though I was in no immediate danger.

In that moment of clarity, I realized the ill-effects of my fear-driven suggestion. I had forced my husband to choose between being loyal to me or being true to himself and the commitment he had made. As I recognized the very honorable man he is, my hurt, anger, and fear immediately diffused.

When we next spoke, I told him: "I'm sorry. I didn't get what you were saying last night. I do now. You were being true to yourself."

He gave me a long, appreciative gaze and said, "Thank you."

How powerful that we can disarm a misunderstanding by engaging our will, intellect, and emotions and choosing awareness, understanding, and compassion.

Chapter 2 - Questions

1.   Are breaches of etiquette experienced in Human Spirit or Human Raw? Provide an example of when you have experienced your etiquette being breached.

2.   Describe one attribute from both male and female team etiquette wiring with which you identify most.

3.   Have you experienced in your own life the difference between male and female loyalty? Describe your experience with both types of loyalty.

4. List one facet of male competition etiquette and one facet of female competition etiquette that surprised you most.

5. Explain the Code of Honor in your own words.

6. How do the men in my study unanimously define honor?

REALITY CHECK:

- When you are in team situations, be on the lookout for the different male and female etiquette wiring attributes.

- Ladies, in conversations with men, practice using both "Is there anything you would like me to know about {fill-in-the-blank}," and "May I tell you about something that really interests me/I care about/am passionate about?"

Chapter Three

Two Tools to Bring Out the Best In Everyone

A re you ready for two more tools to build our understanding of interactions? You see, the point is not just for you to learn this material but to continue adding more tools to your tool belt that will help you live a life where misunderstanding loses, and understanding, respect, hope, love, joy, authenticity, and healing win.

In this chapter, we are creating awareness of Transition Time and Getting Underway—also known as Implementation. We'll unpack these—what they are and how much they impact each of us. The intangible quality we will focus on is supporting people and processes.

Before we go any further, let me answer why it's worth investing time and energy to learn about Transition Time and Getting Underway and how to support both. Everything in this chapter is meant to help you create and hold space for you and those around you to be your best selves. Just think what it would be like to live in a world where we are all equipped with the capacity to be the finest version of ourselves!

Learning about Transition Time helps provide greater connection, harmony, and results. It also equips people to knowingly commit to supporting themselves and those in their lives during one of the hardest things we do, which is Getting Underway. This process ranges from ensuring everyone is ready for school and work each day to initiating the turning of a dream into reality.

Unlike male and female etiquette differences that are sourced by how genders are wired, Transition Time and Getting Underway are not gender-specific. The two operating modes, however, play heavily in misunderstandings that occur. As a reminder, both men and women can and do operate in either mode.

First, we will look at how the survival instincts found in both Gathering and Hunting Modes impact these tools. Women in Gathering Mode are compelled to find positive attention and interest to create connection and be able to answer "Yes" to their driving question of "Am I safe?" Hunting Mode survival instincts, present in both men and women, drive hunters to be single-focused. This focus is an essential element of being successful at producing a result. At an instinctual level, that success equates to both the hunter and those important to them succeeding and surviving.

Remember, women in Gathering Mode experience instinctual tension as they seek positive attention and connection. When this tension runs headlong into the hunter's single-focus survival instinct, it does not bode well for relationships. Unless an affiliation with someone is critical to reaching the goal, the connection, for the hunter, becomes an irrelevant detail that unconsciously gets screened out. This is a "perfect storm" for misunderstanding to transpire.

These conflicting instincts play out in three aspects of each mode—focus, mindset, and how energy is spent.

From Chapter 1, we know people in Hunting Mode have single-focus and naturally screen out details that are NOT RELEVANT to the current goal.

Their mindset is very committed. That commitment focuses a hunter's energy on a specific result, intention, or destination.

We also know people in Gathering Mode have diffuse awareness. All their senses accumulate details because EVERY DETAIL IS RELEVANT. Their mindset is open and uncommitted. They spend their energy collecting every single detail and creating many options, alternatives, and possibilities.

The information in this chapter will hopefully draw in the soul processes of your will, intellect, and emotions so that you can choose to create a response that transports you into living from Human Spirit. There, you can overcome misunderstanding as you live with the awareness of Transition Time and Getting Underway, and learn how to support both.

Now, I'd like you to think of a time when you have been in Hunting Mode and you were interrupted. How did you react? What was that experience like for you? Do you have an image in mind? Is it possibly not the prettiest of pictures? Please put a pin in that experience, because we will come back to it later in this chapter.

Tool #1 - Transition Time

We are now ready to unpack the specifics of Transition Time. We all make transitions throughout each day that involve a single-focus change.

Some daily transitions are:

- Waking up in the morning
- Changing your role from being a parent to being an employee

- Answering a phone call when you have been focused on something else
- Going to a meeting
- Exercising
- Arriving at a restaurant

Some bigger life transitions are:

- Going to college
- Getting a job
- Getting married
- Having a child
- Caring for parents
- Losing a loved one

Transition Time is a function of Hunting Mode. For a hunter to success-fully switch their single-focus from one goal to a different goal, data from the first goal must be pushed out or released, creating space. This zone may be mental, physical, emotional, or a little of all those things. Sometimes, that space is a data feed that requires nothing of the person—no decisions, no responsibilities. That type of input pushes out the previous data, creat-ing capacity for the new focus and facts—like a broom pushes away a mess on the floor so you can start fresh.

One male research panel member described it this way: "We [men] go to a rest stop before we get back on the highway to action. That's called 'checking out.' I can completely relate to that." His specific data feed is his phone. He looks at Facebook or something sports-related.

The diagram below helps illustrate this concept.

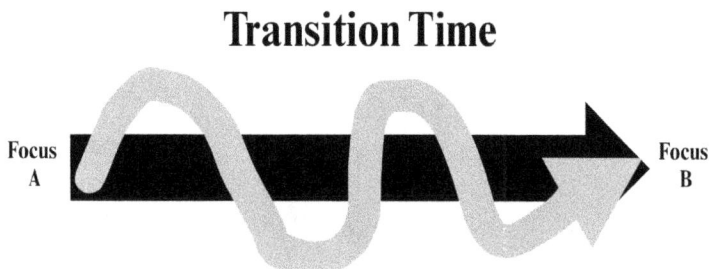

Transition Time

Focus A **Focus B**

Life would be much easier if transitions were as direct as the large black arrow, and we could always go straight from Focus A to Focus B. That would make them easy to recognize and respect. In reality, however, transitions vary a great deal and look more like the curved arrow. The consistent factor for a need for Transition Time is a change in an individual's single-focus.

A woman on my research panel in her mid-sixties described the need for Transition Time when she is in Hunting Mode this way: "My brain is too full of one thing to see what else needs to be done."

A man in his mid-twenties described a simple yet profound lesson he learned as a child from his cat about Transition Time after they moved into a new house. He said, "People just need time to settle in, or they get all hissy."

Not only do people in Hunting Mode require Transition Time, but only the hunter, male or female, knows the specific components needed for their own Transition Time to be successful. One man put it this way when describing interactions with his wife: "Where we have disagreements is how I spend my Transition Time."

Now, I would like you to engage your imagination, or perhaps you have real-life experiences to draw from, as we look at four very common transitions we all experience.

TRANSITION: FROM—HOME. TO—WORK.

After a long weekend of running her three kids around to activities, fixing meals, and doing laundry, Betty returns to work. She has a huge smile on her face, takes a deep breath, and thinks *Hello, work!* Bob is also returning to work after his long weekend, but he doesn't have any children. Instead, his weekend was filled with his favorite pastime. His steps are slow. His heavy sigh and expression are easily read as, *Ugh...this place, again.* Both people had a long weekend, but can you see how the difference in the "FROM" greatly impacts their transition? Keeping that in mind, think about how your personal transition to work each day may vary quite a bit depending on the influence of your "FROM."

I asked a man in his mid-twenties what capacities he loses if he doesn't have Transition Time when arriving at work. He said, "I do the immediate versus the important." I applied my imaginary duct tape and waited to find out if he had anything else to say—he did. "If I don't settle in, I feel like I am part of the river of the moment. But if I am settled in, I feel I have more of a grip and am able to be in a boat. I'm still in the flow, but I have more control, and it feels safer to me."

Which version of this person do you want to employ or have as your coworker?

TRANSITION: FROM—WORK. TO—FAMILY.

This particular transition is so important, but it can be challenging to honor and give space for unless there is awareness and understanding of what both parties can gain.

While conducting research with a man in his early thirties, I asked what he needed to transition from work to family. He said, "I need time to have no responsibility and do nothing." For him, a successful transition occurs when he quickly connects with his wife and kids and then takes 20-30 minutes alone out on his porch. I was curious to know what this provided for him and asked him who he could be if he had that time. He said, "I can be present. I can take genuine interest in the things they want to tell me. I can intentionally love rather than passively."

That's someone with whom I'd like to spend the evening. How about you?

Sometimes, a person will create rituals for their most common transitions. A mid-thirties male research panel member described his usual transition ritual from work to home this way: "My family knows they won't get much out of me until I can shower and recompose myself to be ready for the next moment in life." This particular man works in a shop in the garage of his house, BUT he still needs this Transition Time.

TRANSITION: FROM—WORK. TO—WORK.

No, that is not a typo. Think about it. Most of the time at work, you are in Hunting Mode—producing a specific result. But during the day, those specific intended results change. How do you successfully switch your focus from A to B? If we are honest, these transitions are often not successful or effective. For three decades, my role in corporate America was as an executive assistant to chief executive officers and an event planner. Before I understood the impact of Transition Time, my plan to get the most from every moment of the day was to schedule all-day meetings with lunch catered. However, my research confirmed the error of my method.

One male research panel member in his early fifties worked for a large, established institution. I asked if he could see that his co-workers needed Transition Time. He said, "I think everybody needs it. The problem is we don't often get it." Once again, I applied my imaginary duct tape. He continued, "I think it is a stressor for people because they don't have any time to just catch ten minutes to transition, regroup, and get ready for the next thing." He told me that the only Transition Time during the day he had for himself to "reset," as he described it, was during his lunch. But, sometimes, he didn't even get that because meetings were scheduled over lunch. When he shared that with me, I laughed and confessed my guilt for having been the person in my company who orchestrated that very scenario.

Compare this experience to a man in his mid-twenties who works at a four-year-old start-up company. I asked him this question: "What do you think of corporate cultures that do not allow for Transition Time?" He said, "I think that's a poor attitude. If people try to rush doing good work, push it, and don't allow for rest, that's a great recipe for burnout. It's not helpful or conducive for productivity that is long-lasting."

Part of my responsibilities in the executive suite was managing CEO calendars. Shortly after becoming certified in this topic, I told my boss, "I think we need to intentionally schedule Transition Time into your calendar to help you be the best version of you." I put on my duct tape.

After thinking, he told me, "If you think we need to do it, let's do it."

A few months later, during my annual review, he told me, "You are a master scheduler." He then shared with me that adding Transition Time to his calendar had been a big help to him the past year. Scheduling Transition Time intentionally became our norm. So much so that several years later, when I retired, it was important to him that I teach my successor about Transition Time and how it contributes powerfully to who he can be.

TRANSITION:
FROM—HUNTING MODE. TO—GATHERING MODE.

A mid-sixties man on my research panel described supporting his wife to help her transition from Hunting to Gathering Mode when they have people over for dinner. They both love to cook, but he noticed how agitated his wife would become trying to both prepare the meal and connect with people. He initiated this change: As soon as people begin arriving, he takes over the preparations, finishing up whatever needs to happen to get the meal on the table. This frees up his wife to have the capacity to connect with their guests as they arrive. He gets to provide for the woman he loves and make her happy. She gets to transition and connect. They both win!

As I mentioned in Chapter 1, most of the time, women can switch from Hunting to Gathering Mode very quickly due to high estrogen levels. However, if a woman has been in Hunting Mode for an extended period, it can be a much more difficult transition. A late-sixties female member of my research panel told me, "When my mom died, I went from being a caretaker to all of a sudden not knowing what to do with myself." The way she was able to make this life transition was to get away for a week to the beach. There, she could clear her head and move "from" the past of being in sustained Hunting Mode "to" Gathering Mode, where the future was full of all kinds of possibilities.

During my conversation with the mid-thirties male who works out of his home, I asked what happens when he is interrupted—when a transition is demanded of him without allotted Transition Time. He responded that he loses the ability to be kind. "I really have to suppress my urge to fight back. My initial urge is to fight for my space and for what is important to me at that moment."

Are you starting to see that having Transition Time is important in your life and the lives around you? Great! My friend Erica did, too.

Erica runs a business. She told me that when things pop up that need immediate attention during the day, most of the time, she gets irritated. That is immediately followed by being upset with herself and judging herself as a jerk.

I taught Erica about Transition Time and how it creates space for us and those around us to be their best selves. A few days after our class together, she sent me an email telling me how her life was changing now that she knew about Transition Time. First, she noticed that to do her best work, her brain needed a little break before she moved on to the next thing. Next, she realized that if she gave herself time to go home and do some of her end-of-workday rituals before going to her boxing class, she would get much more out of her class than when rushing straight to her class.

Last but definitely not least, the light bulb went on for Erica that even though she's been pretty good at knowing how important timing is when dealing with other people in her life, she is just now realizing that she would do better if those who need her would consider and respect her timing! Erica saw that her day got off to a difficult start when someone was in her face with a problem before she could even open her office door and put her purse down!

Erica told me, "I understand myself a little better. I know I need more Transition Time between my tasks, and it's OK to need that...I may not be such a jerk after all!"

TRANSITION TIME PARTNERSHIP CHOICES

If we could help each other not be "jerks," would making partnership choices about Transition Time be worthwhile? Personally, I've found it well worth the effort! One simple yet impactful choice I made was noticing and respecting the time my husband needs to transition when he wakes in the morning. I'm one of those people who is ready and set to go when I wake up. My husband is on the opposite end of that spectrum. For a long time, I totally misunderstood his morning demeanor. I took it as if there must be something wrong with me for him not to enjoy jumping into our day immediately. Why wasn't he as happy to see me as I was to see him? This resulted in many rough starts for both of us. When I realized his behavior was not personal towards me, I started allowing him the time he needed to wake up, without interrupting him or diving into our first conversation. The result? The discord disappeared. Woohoo!

One of the questions I asked a mid-fifties male research panel member was, "Do you see the need for Transition Time in the lives of men around you?" He said, "It's probably universal." I was curious and asked him who he can't be when he doesn't get the Transition Time he needs going from A to B. He said, "I will feel more threatened and therefore be more threatening than it is like me to be. It brings out the worst in me."

Do you want to spend time with that person? I don't.

Let's put your imagination to work again. Picture a prima ballerina who is intricately balanced by the male principal dancer. Ballet is actually one transition after another that don't just randomly happen. The dance is intentional and choreographed. The result is amazing. If we choose to be intentional about looking for and supporting Transition Time for ourselves and each other, our results can be amazing as well.

Here are a few ways to be intentional:

- Ask how you can support another person's transitions. That is your choreography.

- Consider whether what you need can wait. Or could you send an email or text rather than interrupting another person's flow? One male research panel member described interruptions of single-focus as "when something comes crashing in." Now, think back to the "pin" I asked you to put in how you have responded to being interrupted. Does this match up with your experience?

- Actively engaging in support and being aware of the impact of interruptions helps create transition space for someone else. Your motivation is to *remember who your affected partner can be* when they have the time to transition between moves.

- Another partnership choice is *figuring out and honoring the Transition Time you need to be your best you.* Like my student Bob did.

Bob shared with me that in the past, he would always hit the snooze button for ten more minutes of sleep in the morning. Then, he would have to rush to get ready for his day. When Bob heard this teaching on Transition Time, he realized that waking up is a form of transition he'd never thought about, and he decided to try something different.

He discovered that choosing to take his time in the morning, giving himself time to stretch, is much more helpful than getting an extra ten minutes of sleep. His snooze button habit caused him to start his day with a lot of stress. He said, "Knowing about Transition Time has helped me be kinder to myself, for sure. Which sets me up to be better to other people and be more productive at my job."

Finally, when you have ascertained the Transition Time choices that will make you the best you, be sure to empower the people in a position to support you with that information.

Tool #2 - Awareness of Implementation

One of the biggest aspects of a transition is Getting Underway. The triangle above is a snapshot of "The Plan" I briefly mentioned while reviewing aspects of male team etiquette. The Plan is the method a person in Hunting Mode believes will provide the best possibility of successfully achieving a specific goal.

Read this diagram from bottom to top. First, a commitment to a result is made, strategizing is completed, and The Plan is formed. Then, it is time for Implementation.

Implementation consists of three parts:

- Collecting Resources
- Getting Underway
- Being Underway

In this chapter, we are focusing on the last two components of Implementation. A male research panel member described Implementation this way: "Implementation is the hard part because that is when the truth gets told. Is all my planning going to work, or is it for naught?" All the men in my research panel agreed that Implementation carries the risk. That is what makes it daunting. A simple example of the risk in Implementation is ice skating. You can read, study, watch videos, and get in shape, but you don't know if you can actually skate until you put on the skates and go out on the ice.

To analyze the difference between Getting Underway and Being Underway, I need you to tap into your imagination again. Picture a NASA rocket launch.

Getting Underway is the time during the launch. The requisite focus of the astronauts is laser-like. Anything less is life-threatening. A huge amount of energy is needed to fuel that focus and withstand the G-forces of take-off to implement the flight. Of course, additional rocket fuel energy must be used to lift the craft through Earth's atmosphere.

Once free of gravity, while still screening out anything irrelevant to the mission, the astronauts' focus is not as laser-like as it was during the launch. They are able to attend to tasks such as media interviews, which provide information and updates to others who have not traveled the stars personally. Additionally, much less rocket fuel is required to keep the vessel in orbit. Both of these changes are indicators of Being Underway.

Implementation is a very specialized type of transition. Similar to previous transitions we've reviewed, it can vary greatly depending on the goal. We've already looked at two very different Implementations—ice skating and rocket launching, a third example demonstrates how long the process of Getting Underway can require.

I asked an early-fifties man on my research panel, "Has it been your experience that Implementation is the most difficult part of any journey, life choice, or ambition? By that, I mean that you have already committed to a specific result, strategized, created the plan, and are now putting all that into action."

He spoke to me for a full ten minutes about a huge work project—leading the complete overhaul of an information systems network for a large company. At first, he described this as a project that had been *underway* for two years. After I shared with him about the energetic phenomenon and intense focus that make up Getting Underway, he completely changed his perspective of the project, *realizing he and his team had been Getting Underway for two years!!*

At the time we spoke, it had been one month since the project "went live." He saw that he and his team had recently shifted to Being Underway. He described the downshift in energy and focus as being so dramatic that he and his team were experiencing adrenaline withdrawal, which is a serious phenomenon. He told me, "There was no breath. It was two years straight adrenaline."

This type of information would be helpful for significant others and families to have, don't you think? Knowing IT IS NOT PERSONAL that their someone special has limited ability—or even complete inability—to connect due to the demands of Getting Underway for a project at work could lead to a greater understanding. When all involved are aware of the energetic phenomenon of Getting Underway and the intensity of focus it requires, we set up a win/win for the person Getting Underway and the people who are important to them. Choosing to mix awareness with the intangible qualities of understanding and support doesn't necessarily make these situations easy to live through, but it can prevent a misunderstanding that may wound everyone and leave possible long-lasting effects.

BE AWARE OF...

As you implement what you've been learning, becoming more aware of how transitions affect you and others around you, be aware of these three phenomena: killing time, doing nothing, and being bored:

KILLING TIME

Killing time occurs when someone in Hunting Mode has transitioned from focus A to focus B and is ready for the next thing, but the next thing or people involved are not ready for the hunter. Both men and women in Hunting Mode are very aware of the resource of time. Not being able to use time productively can be very irritating. A mid-sixties male research panel member described what it's like for him when he has to kill time, "If someone is a half-hour late, I think that is painful. It obstructs your goals."

DOING NOTHING

Do you have a job that is not physically demanding, yet you still go home exhausted from focusing all day? That was my life for decades. When researching this phenomenon with my husband, I laughed when he told me, "You need a 'doing nothing vitamin!'" He continued explaining to me, "I think doing nothing is a very necessary thing. Mostly, what it should be is turning focus off. It's an essential part. It's like a vitamin. You need to do it every day." I've put his advice to the test and can personally corroborate that he is right.

The amount of energy required for the single-focus of Hunting Mode is very significant. Creating time and/or physical space to allow your mind to intentionally wander without having to produce anything is an effective way to decompress and recharge.

When women in Gathering Mode encounter others "doing nothing," it can get ugly if they are not aware of the benefit this practice produces. This misunderstanding stems from the instinctual response inherent in Gathering Mode that considers *getting something done* makes something Worth-It. In Gathering Mode, any undone task is worth doing, as it persistently natters away: "You slob. Fix me, straighten me, put me away, wash me. No peace for you until you do!" It's *obvious to the gatherer* that the person "doing nothing" doesn't care about her. If they did, they would help her with all the things that, from her point of view, clearly need to be done.

Another way "doing nothing" is encountered is when a woman asks a man what he is thinking, and his answer is, "Nothing." Does that answer perplex and maybe even agitate you? Now you know what is happening for both people. Neither person is misbehaving. But misunderstanding is at work, creating havoc.

BEING BORED

The third phenomenon to be aware of regarding transitions is being bored, which is VERY different from doing nothing. Do you recall from our discussion of the Worth-It Calculation that someone in Hunting Mode must get more back than they invest? The investment and the return can take the form of time, energy, money, or a combination of the three. If the return is not more than the investment, the task is not worth the effort. And if NOTHING is worth doing, being bored sets in!! This is undoubtedly an unpleasant experience compared to the relaxation of doing nothing.

Because hunters are acutely aware of how they spend their resources of time, energy, and money, having nothing worth doing feels like losing time that they will never get back. This experience seems to be very wasteful and irritating.

When I asked one male research panel member if it resonated with him that "being bored is having nothing worth doing," his voice and demeanor became very impassioned. He said, "Bored would make me angry! You're alive—there is something worth doing!"

For those of you who are parents to either little or teenage boys, I suggest you deliberately listen to catch when they describe themselves as bored. At their age, testing themselves and finding adventures is what passes their Worth-It Calculation. To avoid being bored, young men tend to search for an activity using those parameters; what they end up choosing may not be the best decision. So, if you hear, "I'm bored," take note and support them in finding something "worth doing."

While teaching this topic to a class, one woman shared an aha moment she was having that beautifully summed up the difference between doing nothing and being bored. She said, "I can do nothing but not be bored!"

GETTING UNDERWAY PARTNERSHIP CHOICES

I'd like you to pull out the image of the ballet dancers we used when discussing the choreography of supporting Transition Time. The points below will help you intentionally structure your dance of partnership choices to bolster successful Implementation.

- **Support according to your partner's agenda.**

  - Always ask, rather than assume, how you can best support someone. How important is this? Compare the answers below of what support for Implementation looks like for two different male research panel members:

    - The first man told me that what makes Implementation easier for him is knowing he has someone to partner with him during the process.

    - The second man told me that what complicates Implementation for him is when he has to sublimate his plan to maintain a connection with the people involved.

  - Do you see how assuming what support looks like could really create problems?

- **Evaluate what you can provide.**

  - After you know what support looks like for someone, use your own Worth-It Calculation to evaluate what you are willing and able to provide. Then, prepare yourself to furnish what you have determined, such as doing a specific task they requested or giving them space and time to implement it on their own.

- **Avoid "killing time" scenarios.**

  ○ Believe and express your conviction to the person Getting Underway that they will get their plan implemented. An early-thirties male research panel member was in the midst of making a life transition. I asked if his wife believed he would get to where he wanted to go. He said, "More than me, honestly." Can you sense the fuel her confidence was giving him?

- **Watch for a shift in energy.**

  ○ Watch for the shift of energy or focus to recognize the transition from Getting Underway to Being Underway. When my husband and I are Getting Underway to go somewhere in the car, I don't interrupt him by talking. I wait until he speaks to me and I sense a change in the intensity of his energy, then I know we have moved from Getting Underway to Being Underway. I asked him what he experiences at this stage. He told me, "A shift in my focus."

Now that you are aware of Transition Time and Getting Underway, what choice will you make for yourself and those around you as life changes and transitions occur? Will you honor that process to hold space for more connection, harmony, better results, responses, and relationships? Or will you fight that process? That choice is always yours.

Chapter 3 - Questions

1. Why would someone want to understand and support Transition Time, Getting Underway, and Being Underway?

2. In your own words, describe what Transition Time is and why it is necessary.

3. From your personal experience, describe a daily transition you make and what support to transition successfully would look like for you.

4. Provide a personal example of Getting Underway that you have experienced. Describe what it was like to shift from Getting Underway to Being Underway.

5. Use one sentence each to compare killing time, doing nothing, and being bored. Provide examples from your own life or the lives of people important to you.

6. Review the four partnership choices to support Getting Underway. Where and with whom could you employ these choices?

REALITY CHECK:

- Be intentional to figure out what Transition Time you need. Share that information with the people it impacts. For three days, commit to exercising Transition Time for yourself. Notice any differences you experience in your quality of life.

- Ask the person you interact with most what Transition Time they need and how you could support it.

Section 2

The Power of Honoring

W hat do I mean by the power of honoring? It's the choice to regard or treat someone with admiration and respect.

Did you notice that nothing in that definition says we must agree with someone to honor them? It's quite possible that, due to your own personal reasons, you disagree with some of the differences between men and women being put forward in this book. However, the time you are taking to learn and understand them is a way of showing respect.

To honor someone is to see them, see their value, and respect them. It doesn't require you to change your beliefs or opinions. That's why it's so powerful. We can agree to disagree and still honor one another. The blame game of "You're wrong, I'm right" loses its power when we choose to appreciate our differences rather than see them as obstacles. We move into observing the uniqueness of each person, not as a threat but as something that adds more depth, richness, and wonder to our lives.

Honoring sets us free to be present in our interactions. Otherwise, we easily get lost as our thoughts wander to evaluating the worth of the person in front of us based on whether we agree or disagree with them. I know that sounds pretty harsh. Yet, take a look at social media. People are quick to objectify and devalue individuals they have never met simply because they disagree. We lose the benefit of our world being filled with the abundance that our differences contribute to one another when we choose not to honor those around us.

Honoring is one of the key intangible qualities in the next three chapters that contributes to unleashing better responses, results, and relationships.

Chapter Four

What's Personal,
What's Not

Thirty-seven years of pain healed. That's the power of what I am about to share with you. I'll reveal that story later in this chapter.

What is personal and what is not in our interactions? Together, we will learn this by unpacking men's stages of development. Understanding and honoring these stages empowers both men who go through these stages and women who interact with them.

I have two goals in this chapter. First, to burst some illusions that women carry regarding who men *should* be. Second, to help men understand they are not alone in the transitions they experience during their lives.

You can engage with this data in two ways: Readily employ the question, "What if there is a good reason for that?" And in asking this, abandon the mindset of assuming someone is misbehaving when you don't understand their behavior.

As we review each stage, connecting the outlined traits to men in your life will help you retain the unique characteristics of each phase.

The foundational pieces of this material are our point of view, how our instincts are at play, the impact of operating modes, and the role of the Worth-It Calculation.

I'm sure you won't be surprised that the facts in this chapter may challenge your point of view. If you feel resistance, please refer to Chapter 1 to help process it. I repeatedly draw attention to your perspective because I am committed to providing you access to the power to change your world. For that to happen, I need you to be willing to look at the part you are playing in the results you are experiencing. Additionally, I am committed to providing information that can improve your quality of life. To do that, I need you to be open to possibly adopting new points of view based on what will be illuminated.

Together, we have looked at how quickly instincts can be triggered. With this information, are you becoming more aware of the tension your instincts can create throughout the day? As we unpack the stages of development of men, we want to increase our ability to recognize the instinctual energy that is triggered by our perception of a threat. What threat might that be? That everything men do or don't do is a personal response. We want to harness that spontaneous power by adding our will, intellect, and emotions. Making that choice equips us to create an awareness about this subject matter and partner it with the intangible qualities of honoring, understanding, compassion, curiosity, and appreciation. This result allows us to live sourced by abundance and partnership rather than scarcity and pain.

Three facets of our operating modes impact this topic. They are focus, mindset, and what makes something Worth-It.

By now, you are becoming familiar with the differences between focus and mindset in Hunting and Gathering Modes. In Hunting Mode, there is single-focus; irrelevant details are unconsciously screened out as the mindset is committed to the goal of the moment. In Gathering Mode, the focus is diffuse and every detail matters, fostering a mindset that is always open to possibilities provided by the continuous collection of more information.

What makes something Worth-It is a focal point that differentiates a man's stage of development. As men transition through growth, their single-focus shifts, which changes the goals to which they are committed, and thereby modifies their Worth-It Calculation.

Ladies, even though this topic is the stages of development of men, you may notice some of these characteristics in yourself when you are in Hunting Mode.

One more thought: While researching this chapter's topic, I asked a man in his late thirties if he saw the Worth-It Calculation at play anywhere in his life. He said, "I'm pretty ruthlessly cutting off anything that I find doesn't add value to my life." Does that help you see how constant and impactful this calculation is to how a man spends his money, energy, and time? If you want to review the Worth-It Calculation before continuing, I encourage you to revisit Chapter 1, which provides in-depth instruction.

Now, we are ready to unpack the specific periods in a man's life. The five stages are Page, Knight, Prince, King, and Elder. The label for each phase was selected from the Middle Ages and is meant to convey honor.

Do you remember our avocado and lime? Each has valuable, unique qualities, but together, they create a spectacular guacamole. Our goal is to honor both men and women for who they truly are. When we do that in our relationships and communication, we gain the ability to complement one another, lifting each other, rather than each gender losing capacities from trying to duplicate the other.

Our goal is NOT to put men into boxes or objectify them. Rather, each stage is a lens through which to see men. As you go forward, never assume you know a man's stage. Because of the uniqueness of each person, the length of time they spend in each phase and the age of their transitions will vary. Instead, use Listening to Learn conversations to gain insight into a man's current stage. Listen for where they spend most of their energy, time, and money—this will help you clarify their current focus, goals, and Worth-It.

STAGE: PAGE

The Page stage occurs from birth to puberty. My research revealed to me that these males are truly "little men." I found it fascinating that, regardless of their youth, their attributes of single-focus, mindset, and employing the Worth-It Calculation were completely consistent with older males.

Their instincts tell Pages their focus needs to be on testing themselves to achieve the Worth-It of discovering who they are. To do this, they focus on fun, adventure, testing themselves, and living in the moment. You can easily see this in how they pick the biggest ball to push when they are toddlers. As Pages get a little older, if they try something, like a sport, and are unsuccessful, they become uninterested in lessons to improve. No, their goal to learn about themselves has been accomplished. They want to move on to the next moment to learn more about themselves by trying something different.

What they need from the adults around them is the freedom to try new things, encouragement to solve their problems, compassion, and opportunities to be the hero. *Asking them for help* to clean up their toys, for example, changes cleaning up from a task that is not Worth-It into an opportunity to be your hero.

Ladies, when Pages encounter problems, you need to check your maternal instinct to make things nice for them—this only frustrates these little men. They want to conquer the problem and win! That is part of discovering who they are. If they seem to get stuck, you can assist them in working through obstacles by asking them, "What do you think you need?" Then, allow them the time to come back to you with an answer. It may take them a couple of days.

While interviewing a ten-year-old Page, I asked what felt so good about being a hero in video games. He said, "When I move on to another level, it makes me feel like I just passed something. It makes me so happy that I passed it!"

During research with a five-year-old Page, he shared about his adventures with his cat and dog. I asked him if he had ever felt like a hero while playing with them. He surprised me when he answered, "No." That made me curious. I asked him, "Who do you think a hero is?" He answered, "I know *what* it is." I just had to ask him, "What is it?" He said, "It is somebody who saves people."

This five-year-old's answer indelibly convinced me that Pages are little men.

STAGE: KNIGHT

The Knight stage occurs from puberty through the mid-twenties or early thirties.

Because his goal continues to be discovering who he is, the Knight's instincts compel him to be intensely focused on pushing his limits through fun, adventure, and conquests while adding the dimension of interacting with honor.

While interviewing a mid-twenties Knight, I asked what a challenge provides for him. He said,

"You're essentially trying to find your limit, really. Where you finally get some pushback and you have to work maybe the extra 20% harder, just to get that goal. Instead of the easy 80%, you need that extra 20."

I asked a knight in his late teens, "What is an adventure to you?" He said, "A rewarding, fun, challenging experience that made me grow. The reward is having completed it and knowing I can do it again."

It's a lot of fun to be around Knights because fun is such a high priority for them. At the same time, Knights can definitely frustrate moms and girlfriends because safety and ease do not appeal to them. You may sense a theme here: men discovering and learning who they are. Knights have no interest in investing their time, energy, and money in what they already know they can do.

Knights have all the same needs as Pages—freedom to try new things, encouragement to solve their problems, compassion, and opportunities to be the hero. Additionally, Knights need opportunities to interact with their honor. When they do this with other men, you will hear comments like "You are better than this" or "I know you can do more." What they need from women to help them interact with their honor is an acknowledgment of the struggle they experience choosing between the right and fun thing to do, such as spending time with a grandparent or watching their favorite sport. Two Knights told me that "seeing the big picture" really helped them determine how to pick the "right" thing over the "fun" thing.

Once again, a caution to women: Soothing does not work well with Knights. Actually, it doesn't work well with any man when he is frustrated. Let him figure it out and solve the problem. If your goal is to be with a man who does not get frustrated, you are searching for a man who is not committed. Is that truly what you desire?

My client, Sally, shared with me that her whole life previously revolved around teaching her son to be the best he could be by allowing him to learn from *her* mistakes. She did that by pouring advice out to him all the time, to the extent that she thought her job as a mother was to make choices for him.

I explained to Sally the instincts Knights have to discover who they are through challenges and adventures. I told her they need the space to do those things and interact with their own honor.

Shortly after our class, her son, Anthony, came home from university for spring break. He was trying to decide whether to accept an internship at Company A or Company B. Essentially, Anthony had his mind made up to go with Company B because his friend had worked there. Sally thought Company A had more long-term opportunities. She was about to tell Anthony that when she remembered he was at the stage where his instincts were driving him to be independent and make his own decisions. So she decided to take a different approach.

Sally waited for a time that was good for Anthony to talk. She told him she trusted his thinking and ability to gather any additional information he needed to make the right decision. The pressure he'd experienced in the past to do it her way was gone. That opened the way for the two of them to continue to communicate with one another about the pros and cons as he went through his decision-making process.

Ultimately, Anthony chose to go with Company A. He explained to his mom that it was because of the long-term opportunities! Sally told me, "This is good stuff. If I treat him like I respect his independence, he ultimately becomes more independent and excels."

STAGE: PRINCE—EARLY PHASE

The entire Prince stage lasts twelve to fifteen years and usually begins in a man's late twenties to early thirties. **There are three distinct phases during this time.**

Again, please use this information as a guideline. During my research, I discovered one man who started being a Prince in his late teens because his life circumstances required him to provide for his family. The uniqueness of his situation helps clarify why we should not use this information to objectify men or try to fit them into boxes. Instead, learn this material, use it as a lens to help you see more clearly, and get curious about the men who are important to you. Look to see how they spend their time. Then, ask them if there is anything they want you to know about that activity. None of this is about agreeing or disagreeing with them. It is about respecting and honoring them by investing time to learn who they truly are.

During the Early Prince phase, adventure is still high on the list of priorities, but the focus changes. The intensity of focus becomes laser-like, shifting to the goal of building his life.

I asked an Early Prince in his mid-twenties, "What does a challenge provide for you?" He said, "Part of the physics in me is problem-solving. When I find a problem that I want to solve and then am able to execute it, it is very satisfying." His answer made me curious, so I looked up the definition of physics. It is the study of matter and energy and the interaction between them. This man defines himself by referencing the way matter and energy interact to solve problems. Pretty intense focus, don't you think?

What makes things Worth-It to men in this phase is finding their fit. This is displayed in their lives as they discover and come to conclusions about what they will build with their life and where they will build. It's not uncommon for an Early Prince to change their school path or job if they are already employed. They are NOT misbehaving. They are searching for their fit. It can be very difficult for mothers and girlfriends to understand this phenomenon. The instinctual drive to feel safe for women sets off "danger, danger" signals when an Early Prince decides to leave a "perfectly good" job or change his major at school after investing multiple years in it. I cannot stress enough how important it is to give men the space they need to make these changes. If men are pressured into "staying put," it can have very unpleasant results when they reach The Tunnel later in life. Keep this thought handy for our discussion about The Tunnel later in this chapter.

A male research panel member in his sixties described the Early Prince phase this way: "I think all men are searching to find their destiny at this age. I know I was."

The drive to find their fit also creates their needs during this phase. The Early Prince needs the people in their life to grant them space and freedom so they can search out and try new things and make changes. If you are an employer, Early Princes need to see a path towards what they want to build, or understand how their responsibilities are contributing positively to what they want to build.

A woman in her twenties heard this teaching shortly before her fiancé made such changes in his life. She shared with me that she was so thankful she understood what was happening. It equipped her to support him rather than judge him as misbehaving and punish him.

Now, a heads-up for the ladies. If you are in a romantic relationship with a Knight, keep in mind that the Prince stage is ahead. Be prepared for his laser-like focus. These men are not choosing to ignore you or anyone else in their lives during this stage—they are simply screening out details that are not relevant to finding their fit and building their life. This happens at an instinctual level, and *it is not personal*. The time a Prince has to focus on a woman or any of the people in his life is a precious commodity. Treat it as such. Don't waste it complaining. If you spend this precious time bellyaching, both people lose. Punishing a man for being consumed with building at this stage makes as much sense as punishing a horse for smelling like a horse.

STAGE: PRINCE—MIDDLE PHASE

The transition to Middle Prince happens because a man has found his fit. His focus becomes even more laser-like to build, build, and build some more. His instincts compel him to achieve his goal of building his life. Anything that is not relevant to accomplishing this goal is automatically screened out. This is not a conscious choice. You may hear him use the expression or his actions described as having his "nose to the grindstone." He simply doesn't look up because he is so driven by his instinct to build.

Due to the time, energy, and money the Middle Prince invests in building, he needs validation and support. Take the time to see how much effort he is putting forth and what he is accomplishing, then express genuine appreciation for those things. Another way for a woman to validate her partner when he is a Middle Prince is via sex. Unfortunately, if women don't understand why the man in their life has so much less time for them, the instinctual female response, which comes from the Human Raw level, is to withhold sex. Remember, women are highly motivated to change if they sense someone is displeased with them. However, for men at an instinctual level, someone being displeased with them does not even register as motivation on their Worth-It scale. Once again, neither person is misbehaving, but both are very much misunderstanding one another.

During this period of their life, men are painfully aware of what they are not providing. They don't need the people around them to complain and point that out. A couple of partnership choices to help negotiate this phase are:

- Ask the Middle Prince, "What would cause you to experience being supported?"

- For a woman to get her needs met, she can say something along these lines: "I understand and respect your intense focus on building your goal. But I also know one of your goals is for me to be happy. How can we work out both of us getting our needs met—yours to be able to focus and build, and mine for attention and interest?" The situation is now framed as a problem—something a man can solve. Give him the time to do so. Men can't do anything with a complaint.

Oh, how I wish I'd known this information for our fourth wedding anniversary. Not knowing caused me to carry the pain of believing I was not enough for thirty-seven years!!

When I got home from work the evening of our anniversary, my husband did not come upstairs to greet me. He is a studio musician, and I could hear him busy working in his home office. His lack of response to my arrival home definitely hurt my feelings, but I decided there was a possibility that he had not heard me come into the house. I went to his studio and interrupted him with, "Did you want to do something to celebrate our anniversary?" He looked up, so startled. It was pretty obvious he had no clue what the day was. He responded with, "Oh, sorry. Where would you like to go for dinner?"

Later, we had barely finished our dinner when he looked at me and asked, "Have we celebrated enough yet?"

I felt literally crushed. What was wrong with me that my husband didn't want to be with me on our anniversary? I didn't know how to express the pain I was feeling. All I could say was, "Sure. Let's go home." As soon as we got home, he went right back to the recording project he had been working on in his studio.

I can now laugh at this comedy of errors and misunderstandings, but at the time, I felt like my heart had been shredded. I never discussed this with him. I was clueless about how to approach that conversation. I was completely unaware that his actions were not personal.

I was incredibly surprised as I researched this topic with him, and, without my saying anything about our fourth anniversary, he referenced that exact event. He told me, "Looking back now at that intense focus can make me, or any man, feel, 'Uh-oh, what have I missed? What did I do unintentionally?'" He continued, "I remember a time you wanted to celebrate, and I asked if we had celebrated enough." I nodded and said, "Yes. Our 4th anniversary."

There was so much healing in that moment for both of us. For the first time in thirty-seven years, I could see and understand that his actions that night *were not about me*! They were about his instincts that were compelling him to build his career, and thereby, build a life for us. My painful self-condemnation of not being enough fell away with no place to attach itself to me. Being able to express the regret he had been carrying about what he'd done unintentionally was healing for him.

STAGE: PRINCE—LATE PHASE

As men move into the late stage of being a Prince, their instincts still compel them to build, but they are also starting to look up a little bit. They evaluate what they notice by asking themselves, *Will this distract me? Will it take away from what I've already built or keep me from reaching my finish line?*

For men to know that all the money, energy, and time they have invested is Worth-It, they have three needs that must be met. Similar to Middle Princes, Late Princes need validation and appreciation. Additionally, they need the people who are important to them to receive what they have been working so hard to build and provide.

Because the three phases of being a prince last approximately 12-15 years, it is essential to be aware of the difference between living out of Human Raw and Human Spirit. I touched on this in the section about Middle Princes; however, the misunderstandings can be so dangerous that I am highlighting this disconnect again.

Women—romantic partners or other family members—living out of Human Raw get hurt and upset by a man's intense focus on building while he is a Prince. They instinctively interpret his actions as rejection. That triggers a response to withhold validation and appreciation in all forms, including sex. Her instinctual response triggers an instinctual Human Raw response in him. Now they are both in pain. Remember, the bottom line for instincts is *How do I outlast you?*—so the outcome is ugly. He has been pouring everything he is into this goal, and he will find a way to get his need for validation and appreciation met. Can you see how the competing instincts, if left unchecked, could drive them apart?

That's why it is essential that both people draw on their soul processes and move out of Human Raw and into Human Spirit. The Human Raw scenario is definitely a scary one. But, if both people intentionally shift to living from Human Spirit, it's amazing what is possible.

I asked a Prince in his late thirties what he could be or provide if he were to receive the support he needed. He said, "I just don't want to leave an inheritance. I want to leave a legacy. An inheritance I can leave physical goods behind, but a legacy I leave pieces of myself behind."

The very last portion of being a Prince is the "sweet spot."

I asked my husband, "When did you first have the realization of the intensity of your focus?" He told me, "I remember very distinctly a spot in time; I can't tell you exactly what age I was. But I know I was in my forties when I actually felt like I took a breath in my thinking, my emotions, and my overall perspective. I felt like it was the first time I looked up in 15 years. Life has been good so far; maybe I should enjoy this rather than attack it."

He was describing his sweet spot. It lasts approximately six to twelve months before the next stage begins.

STAGE: THE TUNNEL

We've seen it in every stage. The essence of a man is an ever-growing certainty of who he is. He has spent his life testing for that, building for that. Suddenly, one day, he wakes up questioning everything about himself. My husband literally transitioned to The Tunnel over a period of a few days. I was traveling on a business trip, running an event. When I left on the trip, he was in his sweet spot. When I called home, it was like the man I knew had disappeared.

The Tunnel is a sacred time, but our society mocks it. This period is marked by the biggest Worth-It Calculation a man will ever encounter.

One research panel member described it this way: "Is what I am doing really me?" The answer to this question for some men is, *NO, this is not who I want to be.* These men turn back to become a Prince and start building something new. Do you remember that I stressed how important it is for Knights to find their fit? This is why.

A man in his mid-fifties provided both ends of the spectrum of coming through The Tunnel. He counsels men professionally and has observed that many men do not come through The Tunnel well. Of them, he said, "Men settle into discontentment and bitterness, and they are resigned to their fate because they built things that are not their identity." But, from his personal experience, he provided a view from the other end of the spectrum—what is possible when a man *does* find his fit. After changing his career three times during his forties, the result when he found his fit was, "I could win at whom God made me to be."

Appreciate and enjoy each stage of development as you go through them with the men in your life—the playfulness of the Page, the adventures with the Knight, and building with the Prince. Be aware of how important achieving his Worth-It is in every stage and how your support and validation empower him to make it through The Tunnel. The gift for both the man and the people in his life is the arrival of a King!

STAGE: KING

Quoting Hermann Hesse (*Siddhartha*, 1922), "The true profession of a man is to find his way to himself."

That is what happens when a man becomes a King. Kings know who they are and are not, what they will and won't provide, and what does and does not interest them. Their focus is to provide for the people in their world and align their world to match their values, the legacy they want to leave, and their relationships.

Appreciation is very important to Kings. They want to know that what they are providing for their realm is making a difference, being used, and being appreciated. That is their Worth-It.

A woman in her late forties made this statement describing her husband, who appears to her to be in the King stage: "There are times I feel he gets irritated when I don't ask for his help."

In addition to appreciation, Kings need the people around them to be curious about who they are and to respect their opinions. They have invested so much into becoming this person. Listening to learn is very important in your conversations with Kings.

Women who are with Kings should endeavor to RECEIVE all the gifts (time, energy, money, opinions, advice) he provides. **If those gifts are not received, appreciated, and/or used, the King will not hang around**. After all, he has invested his entire life building towards this. Please remember, a King offers gifts not because he thinks the woman he is with is unable to care for herself. His motivation is to enhance the quality of her life.

I can speak to this personally. I was diagnosed twenty-seven years ago with Fibromyalgia. When my husband would *try* to help me and care for me, most of the time my internal response was to feel his actions just confirmed to me what I truly didn't want to admit: I was a burden and a problem. Because of that, I would push away his help with responses like "I'm not useless" or "I can take care of myself." That was pretty unpleasant for both of us.

Fast forward to now. When I have a painful day, my King is quick to see it in my body language when no one else does. He immediately asks how he can help me and what I need, not once, but multiple times during the day. My capacity to receive has grown, and I quite gladly accept his help in its many forms. Just the other day, I was feeling much better and happier after his help. He told me, "It makes me so happy when you are happy."

I'd say that is a win/win. How about you?

ELDER—NOT A STAGE, BUT A STATE OF BEING

Lastly, some men develop past being Kings into becoming Elders. PAX Programs, with whom I completed my training and certification, has interviewed thousands of men. Their research indicates that approximately 12% of men transition to the state of Elder.

Three characteristics help you recognize Elders.

First, they are beyond ambition. Their focus is on how blessed they are and how many people have contributed to them.

Second, an Elder needs to know that no one else can provide for a need before they contribute the supply. This is very different from Kings, who are much more intense about providing what they believe the people in their realm need.

Third, Elders empower the people and communities around them by asking questions that make people think. Again, this differs from Kings, who are quick to contribute advice.

Elders need to be appreciated and recognized. These two things cause them to flourish. Their Worth-It is met by calculating whether a commitment is the best use of themselves by the people they love, are passionate about, and to whom they belong.

I was fortunate enough to have an eighty-nine-year-old Elder as part of my research panel. I asked him if he liked to offer advice immediately or if he preferred people to ask him for advice. He said, "Oh, I would rather let them ask for it. I don't feel I'm really qualified to give anybody any advice. I never went to college or anything. All I ever did was drive nails and make sawdust. My good fortune is not my doing. I just accepted good advice."

Oh, by the way, this particular Elder built a company that constructed most of the subdivisions on the west side of Chicago! Yet, his outlook was not on what he achieved but on how much he had been blessed by the contributions of others in his life.

In closing, I asked the above Elder a second question: "Do you see any of these stages in your own life?" He answered, "Well, yeah. I think if you think back, you can see it all."

My hope is that you will choose to use this information about the stages of development of men living from Human Spirit. Partner this awareness with the intangible qualities of understanding, compassion, curiosity, and appreciation. Engaging in this way will empower you and those around you to have better responses, results, and relationships.

Chapter 4 - Questions

1. Name the five stages of development in a man's life. What attribute of Hunting Mode should you look for to identify a stage?

2. How are Pages and Knights similar and different?

3. Outline what changes for Princes as they move through the early, middle, and late periods of being a Prince.

4. In your own words, describe The Tunnel. What does finding their fit have to do with The Tunnel?

5. What three things does a King need?

6. How can you recognize an Elder? Do you know any Elders?

REALITY CHECK:

- What personal insights does understanding men's stages of development provide for you? Are you able to dismantle any past hurts using those insights?

- Ladies, have Listening to Learn conversations with men to help you discover their focus and what's important to them.

Chapter Five

Six Keys to Achieving Goals Without Drama

B efore I learned the contents of this chapter, I had no idea how much I was judging and misunderstanding my husband. For forty-one years, my perspective had been that my husband would do anything not to plan. How wrong I was. More on this later in the chapter.

There are six keys to achieving goals without drama:

1. Commitment
2. Strategizing
3. Build the Plan
4. Implementation
5. Assessment
6. Story Telling

These comprise the structure of The Plan, which I first mentioned in Chapter 2, in our discussion about male team etiquette. Choosing to invest time and energy to unpack The Plan is one more way we can honor each other. Our endgame for this chapter is to come away equipped to honor the process of achieving a goal.

FOUNDATIONAL PIECES OF THE PLAN

The first foundational piece of The Plan is our point of view. Our reality is created by our perspective. As with the other topics, you may experience resistance to this material. You can always refer back to Chapter 1 to help process that resistance.

Another piece is that The Plan is directly connected to Hunting Mode. For that reason, ladies, you may see quite a few of these characteristics in both yourself and the men around you. To move past reacting and into honoring, we must harness our Human Raw instinctual energy using the processes of our soul. This empowers us to create a response from the awareness of this chapter's material partnered with the intangible qualities of understanding and honoring, setting up a scenario for thriving. Wayne Dyer, author and motivational speaker, is widely attributed with a teaching that describes this beautifully; it states that abundance is not something we acquire, it's something we tune into.

By now, you are probably very familiar with the roles of focus and mindset in Hunting and Gathering Modes. Both of these come into play in The Plan.

Nevertheless, I uncovered new information about focus during my research on The Plan. Even though women in Hunting Mode are quite capable of single-focus and successfully achieving specific goals, her single-focus can easily be interrupted by diffuse awareness. However, most men, most of the time, will not experience that interruption. During my research, multiple men described interruptions as "when something comes crashing in."

Additionally, for females, there is the flip side of diffuse awareness resulting from collecting so many details. At an instinctual level for a woman, her consciousness about the details she has collected makes it "obvious" that everything must be, in some way, about her. The term my teachers imparted for this phenomenon is "Center of the Universe." If no one has ever pointed it out to a woman, there is a good chance she is not aware it is happening. As we unpack the parts of The Plan, we'll learn how much mischief the Center of the Universe point of view creates.

I have personally experienced a downside when the Center of the Universe perspective steers my thoughts. Following the path of thinking that everything is about me in some way often leads me to the conclusion that everything bad is my fault. I take on responsibility and blame that is not mine to carry. This is a painful way for me and those around me to live. When I think this way, I tend to withdraw and be short with people.

The good news is, ladies, if you do the math, there is only a 50/50 chance that any particular response or scenario is about you.

A third aspect of the two operating modes we have not yet discussed shows up in The Plan: the instinctual approach to survival.

In Hunting Mode, to achieve the goal of the survival of the individual or tribe, the instinctual response is to conceal strategies, strengths, and weaknesses. This serves as a protection against the information being used to hinder the individual or tribe from achieving the goal.

Another survival instinct seen more often in male hunters is a lack of "trying." Instead, they rely solely on The Plan, believing it has the greatest chance for success and, therefore, their survival. Historically, hunters learned from wooly mammoths, tigers, and marauders that without a good plan, you die. This is definitely a powerful deterrent against simply trying. Does this help you see where the life-and-death urgency that coexists with having The Plan originates?

In Gathering Mode, survival instincts show up in a couple of ways. First, we have previously touched on the life-and-death urgency tied to feeling connected and having the favorable attention of those around you. Second, in contrast to hunters who don't try, gatherers were trained by babies. For the tribe to survive, the baby must survive. For that to happen, gatherers learned to try anything that had even the slimmest chance of success in stopping the baby from crying. They did this for two reasons. One reason was to prevent the tiger from hearing the baby and going after it. The second reason was to meet the baby's needs.

The last foundational piece at play in The Plan is the Worth-It Calculation. This is a very big part of how The Plan is formed and whether it is pursued.

THE PROCESS OF ACHIEVING A GOAL

Assessment   Storytelling

This graphic provides a synopsis of the process of achieving a goal. First, let's do a quick overview of this graphic and follow it up with a deeper look into each stage.

The process starts at the bottom of this triangle—with Commitment. There is no Plan until a considered objective passes the Worth-It Calculation and a Commitment to that result occurs. Once a Commitment is in place, Hunters move quickly to the "how," which is Strategizing. This is comprised of researching all facets of the goal to determine what resources and actions will be required to accomplish the goal. Next, Hunters build "The Plan" by organizing the research results in a way they believe provides the best chance for The Plan to successfully achieve the goal.

Then comes Implementation—putting The Plan into action. As discussed in Chapter 3, this requires a lot of energy and focus. Then, the goal is either achieved or not. That result then goes through an assessment: what worked, what didn't work, what can be carried forward to use again, and what should be discarded. Last is Storytelling. As a teaser, ladies, Storytelling is not what you think! I will elaborate more later in the chapter.

I asked a male research panel member in his mid-fifties if his wife would be surprised to know about The Plan. He said, "Yes. My wife would be surprised that I have a plan. She would also call into question every step of my plan. It totally chills momentum."

Now that we've looked at what is required for committing to the goal and seen a general synopsis of the process, we are ready to get into the specifics of each phase that comes after the commitment. We will look at each phase from the perspectives of Hunting Mode, Gathering Mode, and Partnership.

STRATEGIZING

This is a time period that consists of researching the "how" to achieve a specific "what." Some people are very verbal during this time, soliciting input from people around them. Others can be withdrawn, collecting information from sources like the internet, books, and past experience. It is likely they will not be quick to share that information to avert compromising their success.

Hunting Mode Perspective

I asked a mid-twenties male research panel member what questions he asks when strategizing. His answer provided a glimpse into how much intentionality goes into The Plan. He said, "What do I need? How long will it take? Do I have an effective way to get this done—organize it? Do I have what it takes? Is it sustainable?"

Hunters (male or female) then evaluate the information they collect, taking into consideration their personal values, resources, strengths, and weaknesses. This process also defines and refines the specifics of the goal.

Gathering Mode Perspective

A person in Gathering Mode does not create The Plan. More often than not, they "run into the plan" at some point during its creation, being unaware of its existence and how important The Plan is to Hunters. If the Hunter creating the plan is verbally strategizing, the Gatherer will be thrilled by the word feast forming the strategy. This creates a feeling of connection and safety. If the Hunter is withdrawn to research for The Plan, the Gatherer will feel disconnected and anxious, not understanding the frustration of the Hunter when interrupted while strategizing.

After a Gatherer becomes aware of The Plan, the instinctual tension that comes from the Center of the Universe mindset exerts itself. This results in a Gatherer analyzing The Plan for whether they agree or disagree with it—after all, to her, "it's obvious" The Plan must be about her in some way.

If the gatherer is in favor of The Plan, she will, feeling safe and connected, seek to support it. If, however, she disagrees and perceives a threat, she will squash The Plan with criticism. Ironically, even if gatherers approve of an idea, they often unwittingly squash The Plan by piling on their unsolicited ideas. For example, a man is creating The Plan to paint a bedroom. The gatherer thinks this is a great idea and enthusiastically responds with, "Oh, I love this idea. And, when we move the furniture to paint, we could have the carpets cleaned." This seems like an "obviously" good idea to the gatherer, but to the hunter, The Plan he has created has been ambushed.

Disagreeing and piling on are both driven by the Center of the Universe mindset in action, creating mischief and misunderstanding.

Partnership Choices for Strategizing

Several partnership choices can bring Hunting and Gathering Modes together during strategizing.

First, look and listen for contextual clues. Even if the hunter is not verbalizing a strategy, you recognize they are strategizing by being aware of their actions. For instance, if the goal is a trip—are they looking at maps or travel websites or talking to others who have taken a similar trip?

Second, express *authentic* appreciation when a hunter shares strategy. Remember, a hunter's natural instinct is to *not* share their strategy for fear of jeopardizing success. It is very painful for men when they share their strategy and get shot down without being acknowledged for all the time and effort they have invested. How important is it to verbalize authentic appreciation? A male research panel member in his mid-fifties told me, "When I say, 'Hey I'm thinking about doing this and doing it this way,' I rarely get feedback that is, 'That's a good idea'—almost never get that. The cost of the communication is what stops me from communicating the process."

Rest assured, you can't go wrong if you articulate authentic appreciation when a hunter shares his strategy with you or asks for your input. A mid-twenties male research panel member described receiving support this way: "Assuming the best is what support looks like to me."

A third partnership choice is WOW—which combines both appreciation and support. You can verbalize "WOW!" in response to the idea itself or to the time and energy they've invested in strategizing. Also, WOW can be motivated by the hunter's gift of using choice and Human Spirit to harness their instincts, making themselves vulnerable by sharing their strategy with you. Just be sure to be authentic when you WOW anything.

Vocalizing appreciation, or WOWing, creates the fourth partnership tool: an atmosphere of safety. Who doesn't want to feel safe when choosing to be vulnerable?

A research panel member in his late twenties described how hard it is for him to share: "Most of the time, I process internally. To process out loud feels like an unnecessary step to try to process with someone else. I have to work really hard to include her in that plan."

You can offer safety by putting on imaginary duct tape, Listening to Learn, and articulating your thanks for sharing. An additional way to create safety during strategizing is to *ask* if you may provide input. Honor the response you receive to this question.

Now, think back to the Worth-It Calculation. If The Plan involves you, he needs information about two things to be successful. First, what you need—i.e., what would make a significant positive impact for you, either in who you can be or what you can do. Second, what would make you happy. This data provides the hunter the opportunity to increase the value of their result, *plus* gain the bonus points of making you happy. The strategizing phase is your opportunity to give this information to a hunter so it can become part of their plan.

A final partnership choice for the strategizing phase is asking yourself if this plan involves you. Here's where you have to choose to reign in the Center of the Universe. If the plan he is strategizing doesn't involve you, let it go. Give him the space he needs for his plan.

In both my business and personal interactions, I have a specific way of clarifying "my part" of a strategy or plan. When asked for something, I provide it and then ask, "Does that provide everything you need?" The answer tells me if my part is finished or not.

I asked a mid-thirties woman on my research panel if knowing about The Plan would have helped her in a past relationship that failed. She said, "I don't know that this information ultimately would have saved the relationship, but it might have saved the friendship."

Isn't that worth learning how to partner in the process of The Plan?

BUILDING THE PLAN

After strategizing, Hunters move to building The Plan by organizing the research results in a way they believe provides the best chance for The Plan to achieve the goal successfully.

Hunting Mode Perspective

People in Hunting Mode draw from their strategizing to build The Plan *they* think will work. It consists of their strengths, resources, and values. It avoids their weaknesses. Good or bad, the hunter owns the result.

My curiosity had me ask a late twenties male research panel member, "Is there anything specific that confirms to you that you have strategized enough and it's now a good time to build The Plan?" He told me, "If the feeling or intuition is right enough to act, then I will go ahead and act."

Gathering Mode Perspective

It is common for the gatherer to bump into The Plan because they don't realize strategizing is over and The Plan is being put in place. When that happens, someone in Gathering Mode tends to try to take over The Plan to convert it to HER strengths. She will also push hard to connect via more talking and strategizing.

Can you see how this response to The Plan would not be received well by someone in Hunting Mode? That being the case, let's look at partnership choices to help prevent this disconnect.

Partnership Choices for Building The Plan

Hunting and Gathering Modes each have unique mindsets toward Building The Plan. The following are some options that may help you navigate the path at this stage.

First, use what we learned about authentic WOWing as part of strategizing partnership choices. The reasons for WOW are the same in this phase: the idea itself, the time and energy invested in creating The Plan, and the appreciation that the hunter has chosen to be vulnerable and share The Plan rather than instinctively concealing it.

Second, be safe by applying imaginary duct tape when the hunter is sharing The Plan. Remember, the hunter is exercising trust and respect when disclosing this information.

I asked a male research panel member in his early fifties what it was like to share his plan. He said, "It used to bother me. I'd think — *Why do you need to know what my plan is? Are you going to give me something to do? Because yes, I have a plan, but I don't know why you need to know about it, because it is my plan, and it doesn't involve you.* I would get defensive." Because of the passion in his answer, I put on my imaginary duct tape to wait for anything else he was willing to share. He continued to tell me, "My wife let me know she was curious because she was making a plan for her day but wanted to be available to be part of my plan if I needed her."

A third partnership choice is to be curious about The Plan. I personally learned how helpful this is while interviewing an early forties male research panel member. I asked him, "Am I hearing you correctly—that your plan itself is to be flexible?" He emphatically responded, "Absolutely right! You have to be flexible." I applied my imaginary duct tape to allow him time to finish his thoughts. He continued, "There are people in this world that will take their plan and run it into the ground. It will defeat them in the end."

Until this conversation, I had no clue that a specific way of being could carry as much weight as a desired result. Suddenly, so many misunderstandings I'd experienced with my husband were dismantled. My perception had been that he had no interest whatsoever in being corralled by having to plan. I could now see that The Plan was always to have space for spontaneity. He is naturally creative and, as a studio musician, gets paid to be innovative. I have a strong propensity to plan in great detail; a large part of my role in corporate America for years was event planning. Therefore, I was continually bumping into The Plan to be spontaneous, which has always been so important to him. This awareness has helped me transition from judging my husband as misbehaving to enjoying the flexibility in our lives established by his spontaneity.

A fourth partnership choice is to ask the hunter how you can support The Plan. A mid-fifties male research panel member described what support looked like for him. "First of all, just listening. To be understood and to sometimes hear, 'Oh, that's a good idea.' That would be groundbreaking to me." Can you hear in his response how, when he had shared The Plan in the past, it had been hijacked, interrupted, or squashed?

This final partnership choice applies when you realize a NEED had not surfaced during the strategizing phase. I capitalized NEED because this is not just something you want to throw in or add to The Plan, but something that will make a difference in who you can be. You can address this by asking, "When would be a good time to tell you about a need I have that I've realized is not part of The Plan?" For this to be effective, this questioner must be willing to abide by the hunter's answer regarding when they have the time or ability to receive this new information. When you do share information about your NEED, get right to the point. An example is: "I've realized I need to have stops included in our trips every ninety minutes so I can get out and stretch my back. Doing this will allow me to be in much better shape when we arrive. I'll be able to enjoy our time together."

IMPLEMENTING THE PLAN

Following Building The Plan, comes the real work of Implementation.

Hunting Mode Perspective

During Implementation, a person in Hunting Mode does four things. They collect their resources, collect their power, and follow the processes of Getting Underway and Being Underway. We've already taken a detailed look at Getting Underway and Being Underway in Chapter 3, so let's focus on collecting resources and power.

The resources a hunter collects are those identified as "needed" during strategizing. A mid-fifties male research panel member described collecting his resources this way: "I need to know that there is going to be a win at the end of it, or I won't even really want to try. I need to know that my plan is going to work before I put it into play." Can you hear his Worth-It Calculation at work before he even expends energy to collect resources?

Perhaps the easiest place to witness collecting power is in sports. Male and female hunters will oftentimes visualize various aspects of the competition that's about to take place. You can also see it when a team comes together to rally one another just before they start. I asked a man in his late twenties about collecting power for himself. He provided this very detailed information. "In general, I do a lot of getting in a quiet place, thinking things over—whether that is prayer or doing a quick meditation. If it is a big conversation at work, I will write out word for word what I'm planning on saying and how I expect the conversation to go. I definitely do a lot to visualize everything in my head before it happens or before I try and act."

Now, it is time to tell on myself. Because of my administrative tendencies, I wanted this process of Implementation to be neat, tidy, and linear. Well, it's not. While researching this subject with my husband, he told me, "Most everything I have done has not been carved in stone. I've never had that luxury because my life has just not been like that. To me, life has been up and down that ladder of Implementation."

It became very clear to me that my linear planning approach via concrete timetables left no room to accommodate my husband's Plan for built-in spontaneity. Does this help you see how counterproductive it is to take this information to create boxes to force the people around us into?

Gathering Mode Perspective

When a hunter is collecting resources and power, a gatherer will most likely feel disconnected because the hunter has withdrawn to accomplish these tasks. As the hunter moves into Getting Underway and Being Underway, the gatherer experiences even more disconnect as the hunter turns his focus and energy toward implementing The Plan.

Without the awareness that this disconnect from the hunter is *not* personal, it is not surprising that a gatherer will intrude and interrupt in an attempt to reconnect. As you have probably experienced, this will not go well for either person.

Partnership Choices for Implementation

During Implementation, the gatherer should draw from the strategizing phase what was learned about their part in The Plan. Whatever that part is, collect the resources needed for it. If The Plan does not include the gatherer, that person can collect what they need to take care of themselves while the hunter is consumed with Implementation.

A second partnership choice is for the gatherer to give the hunter the time and the physical and emotional space necessary to implement The Plan.

Third, honor Implementation by being silent and pleasant. The hunter will "come back" and reconnect once they are underway.

I can personally attest to this last partnership choice about Implementation. Before I knew this information, I always tried to "help" my husband when we were leaving the house. I would ask questions like, "Do you have your keys? Did you see your wallet on your desk?"

Almost 100% of the time, shortly after we were in the car, he'd realize he'd forgotten something, then angrily say it was my fault!! His point of view was that he didn't have what he needed with him because I'd interrupted him. From my perspective, I was thinking, *What a doofus! I told you exactly where everything you needed was. If you would only listen to me.* I was clueless that my "help" was crashing into his single-focus on Implementation. The truth was neither of us was misbehaving. We certainly were misunderstanding one another, though.

Now, I prepare myself and wait for my husband to tell me he is ready to leave. Life is much more pleasant and peaceful. We leave the house happy. Who knew???

A final partnership choice for The Plan is a tool called "Time Out."

Before you think I'm setting a double standard, I realize I have repeatedly emphasized the negative impact of interrupting people in Hunting Mode. However, we don't live in a perfect world, and sometimes interrupting The Plan is very necessary. When this occurs, similar to baseball, what is needed is a Time Out. The hunter is too focused to call Time Out on themself. They need someone whom they consider safe and trusted to do this, just as a coach or catcher would do in a baseball game.

You call a Time Out by pointing out to the hunter that either the facts used to create The Plan have changed, or that the facts given when strategizing were bad—incomplete or incorrect.

I asked an early-sixties male research panel member, "Am I hearing correctly that Time Out is a good thing?" He said, "Almost always. It is a way to have the team get the result they want to have."

This tool is not for second-guessing or crying wolf. It is for a genuine emergency. By that, I mean if no changes are made to The Plan, everyone involved will be headed towards a proverbial cliff.

I was very thankful to be aware of this tool when my boss asked me to review an email he wrote about a topic that upset him.

After reading it, I re-wrote the email and sent it back to him because I knew he would regret sending it out in its original format. He came to see me personally to tell me the rewrite was not aggressive enough. It did not accomplish his goal for the team to see how unacceptable their performance was.

At that moment, I realized he and his team were "headed for a cliff" if he sent out his original email. He would not be able to "unsay" the way he'd written his original email and the negative impact it would have. I recognized it was up to me to call a Time Out.

I did that by speaking directly to the point. Saying, "What you wrote is not presidential," this gave my boss a crucial new fact that actually startled him.

This Time Out opened up a powerful conversation about how he could effectively convey the intensity of his message and still be presidential. We sent out our combined third version of the email *and* produced the necessary results.

ASSESSING THE PLAN

This phase encapsulates The Plan in its entirety; its form includes a very large range. It is a conscious Assessment of the whole plan—from Commitment to reaching (or even missing) the Goal. Hunting and Gathering Modes are not relevant at this stage.

Some people do not assess at all. Their perspective looks like, "Ok, done! What's next?"

A very simple form of completing an assessment is observing what worked, what didn't, and what we want to do again. The level of detail and complexity can escalate to corporations spending millions of dollars to assess the results of The Plan.

STORYTELLING

People have used Storytelling as a means of communication for eons, and for just as long, the story's point is often misunderstood between genders. For our purposes, Storytelling, as with Assessment, envelops all of The Plan. I discovered from my research and personal experience that Storytelling is impacted by gender as well as the operating mode. My research showed that the characteristics outlined below are experienced by male hunters and female gatherers.

Hunting Mode Perspective

Hunters craft stories for one of three reasons:

- To recapture energy.
- To teach.
- To establish status (either the hunter's status or the status of someone with them).

Hunters will retell stories many times to accomplish any of the above motives. When they do, things in the stories tend to become bigger and better.

Gathering Mode Perspective

As you already know, people in Gathering Mode are very much about collecting and sharing *details*. When they tell stories, what they are communicating or listening for is "a fact transmission to avoid poisonous berries."

Because of this perspective, gatherers are very insulted when a hunter repeats a story. What the gatherer "hears" is two things.

First, their ability to collect and remember facts is being questioned. The instinctual response for a gatherer is to vindicate themselves immediately. Considering that this repeated version of the narrative will most likely be bigger and better, the gatherer interrupts the hunter by correcting and finishing the hunter's story to prove she heard it correctly the first time. She thinks she has made her point and exonerated herself. Meanwhile, he is simply bamboozled as to why she is telling HIS story.

Second, because a woman's perspective is that forgetting you told someone something is insulting, her thoughts go down the dark road of, *To what other woman did he tell this story, because he obviously doesn't remember it was me!*

But the misunderstanding does not stop there. The difference in the details also sends up a danger, danger flag in the instincts of a gatherer. For example, she knows the story took place on a Wednesday evening, but he just said it was on a weekend. Her thoughts get even darker with something along the lines of, *If he would lie about this, what else would he lie about?*

It's not too hard to see that the hunting and gathering instincts are totally at odds when it comes to Storytelling. Neither perspective is right or wrong. They are simply different. And both perspectives are important for survival.

That's why partnership choices are so important and powerful when it comes to Storytelling.

Partnership Choices for Storytelling

First, encourage Storytelling. Watch as the man recaptures the energy and refuels. By Listening to Learn from stories, you can draft off this energy.

Second, remember hunters craft stories for one of three purposes: to recapture energy, to teach, and to establish status. When a hunter tells a story, he is NOT doing it to transmit facts.

Third, listen for the point of their story—energy, teaching, or status.

Fourth, be curious. If the story is about recapturing energy from an experience, what is motivating them to gather that energy? If their story is about teaching, what point are they teaching, and to whom? If the story is about status, is it about their own status? Or are they deferring status to another person?

One man described the point and purpose of storytelling to his wife when he arrived home from work: "When I tell my wife stories about my work, I'm peacocking to remind her I can provide for her."

When I interviewed my 88-year-old father-in-love in 2018 about this entire topic, the conversation became full of stories about his life. He had become a widower in 2016, and it had been a very long time since I'd heard him that animated. Experiencing how telling stories recaptured his energy changed how I interacted with him from then until he passed away in 2021. No longer did I check for a "factual report" such as "How are you?" or "What happened today?" Rather, the time we shared was filled with new and repeated stories he told me. My encounters with him permanently changed how I listen to all men and the stories they tell.

A famous, real-life example I can offer you about the difference between storytelling and "fact transmissions" is from *The Sound of Music*[1]. The year was 1938. Captain Von Trapp and Maria were faced with a specific problem to solve. What would be best for his children? You can easily search the internet to learn that the movie is not a "factual transmission." But it is their *story* of conflicting instincts that evolved into an incredible partnership.

Chapter 5 - Questions

1. In your own words, describe the survival instincts in Hunting and Gathering Mode that clash within The Plan.

2. What are the six facets of The Process of Achieving a Goal?

3. Explain the Center of the Universe in your own words. Provide examples where you have seen it or experienced it.

4. What does WOWing authentically provide? List things to WOW. In what phases is this tool used?

5. When and how do you use a Time Out?

6. What surprised you most about Storytelling? Share a time from your own life when you experienced a Storytelling disconnect.

REALITY CHECK:

- Take the time to watch the movie *The Sound of Music*[2] and look for where you can identify The Plan weaving throughout this film.

- Ladies, consciously check yourself for how you listen to stories.

2.

Wise, R. (Director). (1965). *The Sound of Music* [Film]. Argyle Enterprises, Inc.

Chapter Six

Three Tools
to Transform
Conversations

B eing equipped with the tools we are about to uncover transformed what could have been a hurtful, explosive conversation between my husband and me into a beautiful gift. I'll share the details of that story with you at the end of this chapter.

First, let's create awareness of how to speak to one another to honor our differences. The intangible qualities required to live out this consciousness are kindness, generosity, empowerment, connection, and cooperation.

The information in this chapter is no different from the others in that your point of view about how you will interact with it is always your choice. If you have thoughts like *Why should I change for them?*—I encourage you to return to Chapter 1 to help you understand your resistance. Adopting different viewpoints is always about creating a better quality of life. It is not about people pleasing. Now may be a good time to ask yourself if you have experienced any changes in your perspectives that have enhanced your results, responses, and relationships from the material in previous chapters.

FOUNDATIONAL PIECES FOR
TRANSFORMED CONVERSATIONS

You're probably not surprised that we will begin our discussion on transforming conversations by examining how our instincts impact our conversations. Do you know why we need to look at this? You are correct if you respond that instincts are our natural reactions and happen quicker than cognitive thought.

The specific female survival instinct that strongly impacts conversations is driven by the question, "Am I safe?" Do you recall that gatherers at the Human Raw level try to create safety by collecting and sharing every detail they can? This was literally necessary to help gatherers and their tribes survive. My nickname for this is "poisonous berry report."

Compare that to the Hunting Mode survival instinct, which is strongly driven by single-focus and screens out irrelevant details, to produce a result that enables everyone to survive.

It's not too hard to imagine how operating solely out of these instincts in Human Raw could result in some very adversarial conversations.

The point of the information in this chapter is to provide a viewpoint that will allow us to:

- Harness the energy innate in our instincts.

- Use our soul's processes to create responses from the awareness of what's possible when we train ourselves and others to give just the right amount of detail to **empower problem solvers** and **create greater connection and cooperation**.

- Partner that awareness with the intangible qualities of kindness and generosity.

Mixing these things provides the recipe to live from Human Spirit and its abundance, and equips you to partner with yourself and those around you. Everybody wins. Sound good?

A male research panel member in his early thirties shared this beautiful example of living from Human Spirit when his wife comes to him with a problem. He said, "Either way, it's a win. If she comes to me with a concise, 'Here's the problem, I need your help,' that's a win. But, it is also a win if I get challenged to be a better person, a better listener, and more patient."

The next foundational piece is how operating modes impact conversations.

Look for how focused a person is as your tip-off about their current mode. Whether conversing with a man or a woman, recognizing Hunting or Gathering Mode will definitely smooth your communication path.

Regardless of gender, someone in Hunting Mode will want you to get to the point as quickly as possible. If you do this, you will connect much more quickly to the hunter in your conversation. You are also creating a win/win for both hunter and gatherer. The hunter gets the point; the gatherer gets connection.

To improve the quality of our conversations, we will compare four attributes of the two modes—focus, listening, the mindset about problems, and safety.

Someone in Hunting Mode is single-focused. If you appear to be fine, they listen for the point; if you appear to be anything other than fine, they listen for the problem. They view problem-solving as a very good thing, as it helps to achieve the goal. Hunters experience safety by successfully producing either the result of the point or solving the problem.

A male research panel member in his late sixties described his experience of listening for the point or problem when it is not provided. He said, "They want me to know what's wrong when they don't know what's wrong. That causes significant frustration."

An individual in Gathering Mode has diffuse awareness. They look and listen for every detail. They collect all these details to share them, confident that distributing this information helps anyone and everyone. They view problems as *bad*. The reason is that having a problem, or even worse, *being* a problem, could cause a break in connection with the person or people around them. Gatherers diligently try to avoid whatever might create a disconnect. Their ability to experience safety via connection and sharing details is derailed if detachment occurs.

While researching this particular topic with my husband, I asked him that if I'm always supposed to get to the point, what am I supposed to do with all the details I've collected so I don't explode? He very calmly looked at me and said, "Make a detail-dump the POINT!"

Now we have a common language. We both understand that when I say I need a detail dump, I'm asking him to hold a virtual trash can for me.

We have some basic ground rules for these types of exchanges.

- I am free to dump my overload of details into a virtual trash can he holds for me. This creates a greater capacity to be a better me.

- My part is to NOT hold him accountable for anything I say during this dump. This means I agree not to use this time to convey information that requires him to take action on it.

- His part is to continue to ask me, "Anything else?" until I tell him I'm done.

- His part is NOT to solve anything.

- His part, when I'm done, is to throw the trash away and not hold me accountable for anything I've said. A woman can never know for sure what might come out when the floodgate of details is opened!

Ladies, you can also use detail dumps when interacting with other women. Obviously, this tool can be used in one-to-one conversations, but it can also be modified for a group situation. A meeting of all women can be started by allowing participants to partner in groups of two or three; give each person one minute to "dump details" or "empty their basket" of what might be consuming their thoughts. This is a very specific way to help attendees transition and be more present for the meeting at hand.

Our foundation for better conversations is now in place, and we are ready for our first tool.

TOOL #1 - THE IMPORTANCE OF THE POINT

Simply put, the Importance of the Point is driven by a hunter's instinctual need to produce a result to be safe. It's impossible to produce the result if you don't know the point.

Male hunters experience the frustration of not having the point much more intensely than female hunters. The reason for this is their inherent higher testosterone levels, which escalate the magnitude of their single-focus. This doesn't mean women don't experience irritation when they are in Hunting Mode and are told lots of details with no point. A female research panel member in her mid-thirties described her experience as "I know I could answer their question if I just knew what the question was."

If no point is provided, out of frustration, hunters will interrupt and ask for it. Immediately, the gatherer's instincts resound, "Danger, danger." The gatherer experiences being thwarted in trying to provide details that, to them, feel life-or-death important. At the Human Raw level, both people believe the other person is misbehaving, which is not accurate. What is actually taking place is a misunderstanding of one another.

To avoid hunters being annoyed and gatherers feeling unappreciated (or even threatened), a simple solution is for the person talking to tell the hunter how to listen up front. This is done by stating the point, the problem, or that what you are about to share is a detail dump. When I asked a late-twenties male research panel member what it would be like for him to be told upfront how to listen, he said, "That would be super helpful, extremely helpful! Once I get that right off the bat, it's like, 'OK, sweet. I know exactly what to do.'" Can you hear the satisfaction in his answer because he knows the result he needs to produce? I wish you could have also heard the relief in his voice when he answered me! I asked this man and several other research panelists if they would hesitate to ask for any details they needed. It's a short answer: "No."

It can be difficult for estrogen-based people to understand that if they have credibility with the hunter who is listening to them, no details, including examples, are needed. I personally experienced this with my boss.

I shared the point immediately by telling him, "I've recently learned about Transition Time and how it helps people be the best version of themselves. I think it would be a good idea for me to specifically include Transition Time in the scheduling I do for you."

I put on my imaginary duct tape and did not provide any details or examples. When he answered, he said, "If you think we should try it, we'll try it." I'd been managing my boss's schedule for three years when we had this conversation, so I had built credibility with him.

Knowing the point impacts who men can be and how they show up. I asked a mid-thirties male research panel member who he could be if a woman got to the point. He said, "I can know who to be in that scenario." His answer made me curious. I just had to ask him who he *can't* be if a woman does not get to the point or problem. His answer was, "I can't be a woman, and that's probably what she needs in that moment!"

A hunter's need to know the point or problem is not limited to adult interactions. It also comes into play relating to children. I asked a male research panel member with three small children what it is like for him when his kids can't or won't get to the point. He said, "I get frustrated pretty quickly." It seemed he had more to say, so I put on my imaginary duct tape and waited. He continued, "I have kinda created a Rolodex of what could be the underlying problem that is making it such a big deal that we can't do this one little thing."

Are you able to recognize in his answer that his frustration stems from not being able to produce the result his children need? The outworking of his love for his children is demonstrated by his creativity in building a Rolodex of possible ways to provide from his previous experiences. He is doing his best to problem-solve without knowing the point or problem.

It's time to draw on your imagination again. Picture pouring out a 1,000-piece jigsaw puzzle over a hunter without giving them the puzzle box. For our purposes, all those puzzle pieces are details. I asked a mid-thirties male research panel member what he experiences when flooded with details without a point. He said, "I hate that feeling of—Am I fixing? Am I listening? Are you wasting my time? Is this about connection? What are the rules to this conversation?"

For this man—or any person in hunting mode—receiving copious amounts of details without knowing the point or problem is extremely nerve-wracking. Depending on the hunter's relationship with the person generating the details, they may be worried about being tested on remembering all these details. Without a structure to organize the details, their eyes glaze over as they think, *How will I remember all this?*

This agitation is created by Hunting Mode instincts at work.

- They don't know the point, which means they can't be successful at producing a result because they have no idea what that result is.

- At the Human Raw level, being disempowered in this manner seems like a threat to their survival.

- It is important to note that the **hunter's agitation is about the SITUATION** in which they find themselves. It is **NOT personal towards the gatherer**.

I asked two male research panel members to provide a metaphor of what it is like for them to receive details with no point. Their answers were:

> "It's like an oscillating fan blowing.
> Something that is directed at you, continuous,
> but it is just a constant noise that doesn't make any sense."
> –early-forties male

> "It's like trying to land a plane, but
> you can't because of turbulence."
> –late-twenties male

While investigating the agitation of the hunter's experience, I made a surprising discovery consistent across all my interviews. How hard and intensely a hunter pushes to discover the point is directly related to how much they care for the person with whom they are communicating. Before learning this, my point of view had been the polar opposite. I thought my husband was interrupting me because he didn't care about me or what I had to say. Yet again, misunderstanding was working its mischief.

I first uncovered this new perspective while researching with my husband. My initial question to him was how he reacted when a woman provided lots of details. His answers were vague and situational. I changed my question to "What's it like for you when I don't get to the point?" His entire demeanor changed. He leaned in close to my face and intently told me, **"I want you to get to the point as quickly as possible so I can help as quickly as possible."** The dramatic change in him inspired me to ask every male research panel member if the amount of energy they expend to find out the point is directly related to how much the person means to them. Yes, was the unanimous answer.

Below are some partnership choices you can make about speaking to the point.

First, provide options to the person listening by asking what they need most—the point or the story. I asked an early twenties male research panel member, "Would it be wise to ask what you need at this moment—the point or the story?" He answered, "Yes, I think that would be great to have at the forefront. Sometimes the story is the point."

Second, if you are a female speaking to a male hunter, start with, "May I tell you something that makes me happy (joyful, etc.)?" You just gave the point to the hunter so they can relax and listen to the details.

Third, honor what the listener wants. Only the person listening knows their capacity at that moment in time. They may have had a very demanding day and only have the capacity to hear the point. Or, they may be relaxing with a glass of wine and would enjoy listening to a story.

Fourth, be generous and kind. Rather than spending a hunter's time giving details they don't need, it is a generosity of Human Spirit to provide male or female hunters just enough information for them to know the point of what you are saying, trusting that if they have questions, they will ask. Show them the puzzle box picture at the very beginning of the conversation by using statements such as: "This is what I need," "This is what I want to share," or "This is what I need you to know."

Acting this way is a kindness, because it allows hunters to experience safety by knowing the result to produce. I specifically asked an early twenties male if it would be a kindness to speak to the point or problem first. He said, "Yes! Both a kindness and a helpful tool."

TOOL #2 - BECOME COMFORTABLE SPEAKING TO THE PROBLEM

We start by remembering that the default listening posture in Hunting Mode when speaking to a person who appears to be anything other than fine is, "What's the problem?" A hunter's thoughts become consumed with a litany of questions as they hunt the problem: *Is that the problem? Am I the problem? Is this the same problem we've always had? Is she the problem? Is this a new problem?*

As if that is not messy enough, when researching this topic with women, I asked, "Are you comfortable telling someone you have a problem?" A couple of their responses are below.

"I probably default to 'I have a question or challenging situation.'
I probably don't use THAT word."
–mid-thirties female

"It's amazing how many times we think we are the problem,
rather than asking, 'What is the problem?'"
–late-thirties female

If you think of this from a supply and demand perspective, hunters inherently demand to know the problem, but the supply is not available because gatherers are so reticent to even acknowledge a problem. This is definitely a scenario rife with opportunities for misunderstanding to occur.

My own experience and my research corroborate that **women associate having a problem** with **being a problem.** Human Raw instincts rapidly react to that perspective with thoughts of *DANGER—you will be unsafe and unwanted if you have a problem.* All this happens more quickly than cognitive thought and creates anxiousness.

Compare this to how men experience problems. I asked a late-sixties male if he liked problem-solving. He jumped right over the word "like" and responded by saying emphatically, "I AM a problem solver!"

To help solve this communication problem (pun intended!), I asked a late-teen male research panel member how, if he had his way, someone would speak to him about a problem. He said, "People would approach me and be transparent, direct, to the point, without trying to soften what they are saying or trying to get to it in a roundabout way. When they are vulnerable, that makes me feel more comfortable being vulnerable in response."

For all my female readers looking for connection, this man just provided one of the keys!

During research time with a late-thirties male, I proffered this question: "What was it like when a woman was upset and you asked her what was wrong and she replied 'NOTHING!'?" He answered, "I can't even imagine a scenario where a woman gives that response and it actually means 'nothing.'"

Being authentic, I have done exactly this. My husband's frustration in those moments has been very similar to the frustration I heard in this man's voice when he spoke. I very much wanted to understand this dynamic, so I discussed it in detail with my husband. I was shocked as I discovered how much misunderstanding was occurring between both people.

Ladies, you may think you are "punishing" a man by responding "nothing" and distancing yourself. At Human Raw level, this seems *obvious* to a woman since breaking off a connection would equate to punishment to another woman. Actually, we are the ones who lose when we do this! Remember, men are literal. We say "nothing," and out of respect, men leave us alone and don't pry. This expression of respect is a product of hunting instincts at work. In this case, it is the instinct to conceal information, thereby not compromising their ability to achieve a result. To a hunter, that equals safety. This ties back to the Code of Honor we discussed in Chapter 2. A man won't ask, pry, or intrude because he wants you to be safe. The mindset is, *If you want me to know something, you will tell me. I'll be respectful and wait until you do.*

What I'm about to say is very important, so please read it, then go back and read it again.

A man leaves you alone and does not pry when you say "Nothing," not because he *doesn't* care. It is just the opposite. Leaving you alone is his way of expressing his care and respect for you.

Why am I putting so much emphasis on becoming comfortable with speaking to the problem? Because our world is full of unsolved problems. What would be possible if we embraced and celebrated all the problem solvers around us? What potential could we unlock if we equipped men with the point and the problem?

Here is what four male research panel members told me when I asked them who they could be if they knew the point or problem:

"Someone who can be helpful to them.
Be a mediator and be kind."
–late-twenties male.

"You have to really know what the problem is before you can fix it,
or you can do more damage than good."
–late-sixties male.

"I can be a support, comfort, active listener, a safe place."
–mid-forties male.

"I love it. It calls me up to a place of maturity.
It validates my dignity.
It makes me feel trusted."
–early-thirties male

Sounds like communicating the point or problem could make the world a better place, don't you think?

TOOL #3 – KNOW THE DIFFERENCE BETWEEN
OPINION, ADVICE, THOUGHTS, INPUT

To use what we've already learned in this chapter, the *point* of this third tool is that you will hear these four words—opinion, advice, thoughts, input—when you speak with men about problems. For men, these four things do not carry the same definition or weight that they typically do for women. Reflect on what we discussed in Chapter 1: Men are literal.

For a woman, opinions and advice can be seen as the same thing. Not so for men. Men form their opinions based on their values combined with a lifetime of trusted facts they have accumulated. A late-thirties male research panel member described his opinions this way. "I have my own matrix between my faith and my experiences that qualify all the parts of my opinions." I put on my imaginary duct tape and waited for anything he might add. He continued: "I've actually found it is important to know my opinions so that I have a good compass rather than a good map."

When asking men about the word "advice," there was a consensus that the difference between a thought-out opinion and advice is that opinions are personal guidance mechanisms, and advice is for the benefit of others. My husband explained the distinction this way: "Opinion is how you form yourself and what you keep, which allows you to give out advice. One is a result of the other."

Why is it important to understand the difference between opinion, advice, thoughts, and input? Because one of these is a man's way of sharing the best part of himself. The only way to find out which carries the most weight for a specific man is to ask him, "Which of these four words is you providing the best part of yourself?" You will need to give him time to think about it. He may need to come back to you as part of a different conversation.

Once he provides his answer, whichever of the four it is, do two things:

- Don't ask him for that particular thing unless you plan to act on it or use it.

- Each time he provides that particular thing for you, treat it with great respect.

After finding out from an early-forties male research panel member that his opinions were the best part of him, I asked what it was like for him when someone did not use the opinion he provided. He said, "I'll tell you exactly how it felt. It hurt." A different man was even more succinct in his response, "It's insulting."

An 88-year-old Elder shared with me that his advice was the best part of him. I asked him if he would continue to provide his advice if it wasn't used. He said, "If they aren't going to take your advice, why bother to give it to them?"

The responses from the research I completed showed a pretty even split between opinions and advice being the best part of themselves. Only one man told me it was his thoughts. Input didn't seem to carry much weight with any of the men with whom I researched.

Partnership Choices for Speaking to the Problem

To help you in your interactions, here are some partnership choices you can make about speaking to the problem.

First, if the person you are speaking to is not the problem, tell them upfront so they are not listening from a defensive mindset. Own your problem if the person you are speaking with is not the problem. Hunters, both male and female, look for partners who do not make them the problem. This holds true for both business and romantic partners.

Second, give hunters the benefit of the doubt about why they are pushing to know the problem. Remember that how hard they push is directly related to how much they care about an individual.

Third, let the person you are speaking to know what help you want.

- Are you looking for input you can consider as you make your decision? If so, you can say something like, "I'm collecting information to help me decide about {fill in the blank}." This alerts the hunter to the fact that you may or may not take action on what they provide. It allows the hunter to decide whether they want to provide the best part of themself.

- A variation of this is to tell the hunter what you have already done in trying to solve your problem and ask them if they have anything they think you should also consider as you come to a decision.

- Or, you can ask for help by asking them to solve the problem for you. This would be me when it comes to plumbing problems! When you ask for help this way, be sure to act on the information provided.

Fourth, don't assume the other person's motives. A late-twenties male research panel member watched his brother's marriage fail because both people assumed the other's motives. He began to understand what was happening in his brother's life from a teaching by Bill Johnson, Bethel Church, Redding, CA: "We are at our worst when we assume another person's motives."

I want to share a story with you about assuming the motives of others. A friend of mine, Debbie, has been married for over 40 years. She shared with me that, for the most part, her life had been filled with a lot of bitter thinking combined with a real sense of hopelessness. She believed she was trapped in an endless cycle of miscommunications. Debbie's point of view that men constantly misbehave caused her to feel that change was simply impossible.

While learning about speaking to the point and to the problem, Debbie experienced moments of illumination when we discussed two things. First, how a man demonstrates respect by not asking more questions when a woman's answer to "What's wrong?" is "Nothing." Second was when she heard the Bill Johnson quote: "We are at our worst when we assume another person's motives." These two aha moments opened up a whole new perspective for her about her relationship with her husband.

Suddenly, it was clear to Debbie how much time she'd spent in needless pain and emotional drama. When she'd answered her husband's question, "What's wrong?" with "Nothing," and her husband did not prod her with more questions, she assumed he just didn't care. Through this teaching, she realized that her "Nothing" left her husband with no problem to solve and no point worth pursuing.

Debbie shared with me, **"I've made the choice to stop the insanity of not communicating the problem when there is one."**

That choice is unfolding a lot of changes for them. She now sees many ways her husband loves and cares for her that she could not see when she assumed his motive. It's clear to her now how much he respects her. She sees his willingness to help her and provide for her during some challenges they are experiencing. And he is opening up to her a little more about his inner life.

Debbie no longer thinks change is impossible. She told me, "These glimpses of change are all in the beginning stages. But, there is a VERY REAL SENSE that change can and is beginning to happen. That's exciting! Whoo Hoo!"

A quote widely attributed to Albert Einstein is, "The world we have created is a product of our thinking; it cannot be changed without changing our thinking." Debbie's world changed because her thinking changed. Are you willing to alter your thinking by speaking to the point and to the problem to transform your world? When you train yourself to give just the right amount of detail, you can empower problem solvers and create greater connection and cooperation.

In my own life, I've been guilty of rudely interrupting my husband because I had quickly judged him as misbehaving. One of my biggest triggers was when I was trying to share details, including my feelings, and he would cut me off with his wanting to know the point or problem. It was pretty predictable that what followed would be a huge fight.

That's what makes what I am about to share very surprising in a good way.

I was in shock. I was at work finishing up a week of long hours and high demands. My phone rang; it was my doctor's office telling me I needed surgery ASAP to investigate potential cancer.

When I got home, my mind was consumed with this news and concern about how I would manage the meeting I was planning for 120 people three weeks later. I was in the middle of trying to share my overwhelming feelings about all of this with my husband when he interrupted me with this statement, "Just stop the crying. We have a problem to solve and an hour to solve it."

I could feel rage welling up within me, trying to take over me. I chose to take a deep breath to help move from Human Raw to Human Spirit. That breath gave me space to remember that the person in front of me was not my adversary. He was a man who loved me deeply. Another deep breath helped me to recall that the intensity of his response was driven by the intensity of how much he cared for me. Both these revelations created the capacity in me to be able to actually hear how he was protecting me and what he wanted to provide for me when he said, "You know, YOU ARE THE PRIORITY. Your company will just have to work out getting done what needs to be done." Everything slowed down for me. I remembered a quote from my instructor, "What if you were special-ordered? What does your world lose if you don't honor yourself first?"

I saw it. My husband was trying to protect me from myself. How beautiful is that? He knew very well I tended to make everything except me my priority. The first step in solving the problem in that hour before he had to leave for work was setting our priorities. Suddenly, we had a plan for how to move forward. We did. Through every test, result, and change made, my husband's focused determination gave me strength. When he told me, "This is an opportunity to find a new road for a better quality of life for you," it became so clear to me that I was *not* the problem; rather, *we had* a problem to solve.

I shudder when I realize I would have missed this incredible gift of love and support if I had judged him as misbehaving, shut him down with my rage, and distanced myself from him.

I had to choose to alter my thinking to be able to receive this blessing. What choice will you make?

Chapter 6 - Questions

1. What Hunting and Gathering instincts conflict with one another when it comes to speaking to the point or the problem?

2. In your own words, why do hunters demand the point? And what drives their intensity?

3. What is a detail dump? Describe how to use it.

4. Have you ever responded "Nothing" when asked what was wrong? Or, have you ever received that answer when you were the one asking? How did those experiences work out for you?

5. What four words are commonly encountered when speaking with men about problems? Why is it important to understand the distinction between them?

6. Are you willing to alter how you speak to the point or to the problem? If yes, come up with a couple of ways to help yourself make this change.

REALITY CHECK:

- Practice using the detail dump tool with the people in your life.

- Ladies, make up sentences that include the word problem in them. For example, "I have a real problem with the word 'prob lem.'" Repeat the sentences out loud a few times. Do you notice any tension in your body as you use the word "problem"?

Section 3

The Power of Harnessing

The definition of harnessing is "to bring under conditions for effective use."[1] What do we need to learn to harness and put to good use? Our differences. That is not always an easy choice to make, and, from my own experience and watching others, I can assure you that you won't always make the best choice, but being perfect is not the point. Whenever we choose to see differences as opportunities, we create conditions that allow us to harness our differences effectively.

You have already received a lot of information about the differences between men and women in the previous six chapters, and there is still more to come. Harnessing and implementing all you have learned will create a better quality of life. The bonus is that as your life changes for the better—with less hurt and misunderstanding—your "dance steps" with those you interact with also change. I experienced this in 2014, within the first couple of months of taking my initial class.

The first weekend, our instructor taught us that change in the people around us will not be instant. Why? Because of all that had transpired in the years prior. Simply *telling* someone "I've changed" doesn't hold any weight. We have to *live out* the change as consistently as we can for them to see it.

1. http://www.dictionary.com

I originally experienced this by how I routinely entered our home when I arrived from work. Our house is ranch-style with a walk-out daylight basement, which is the location of my husband's office. In the past, I would simply barge into his work area, without considering how my actions would impact him. The closest outside door to where we parked happened to be the door to his office, and because it's my house as much as his, in my mind, I "should" be able to use that door. I'm sure you won't be surprised that, instead of giving me the warm welcome I wanted to feel, my husband was usually short with me upon my arrival. Misunderstanding, I interpreted this as more evidence that we were growing apart.

Having learned how interruptions are so negatively impactful for someone in Hunting Mode, I chose to "harness" this difference by walking around to the front door of our house rather than interrupting him. I did not say anything to my husband about my decision to alter my routine. Instead, I lived it out.

After a few weeks, he commented that he noticed I was no longer coming into the house downstairs. I told him what I'd learned about how disruptive interruptions are for him, and that's why I chose to change. He looked surprised, with a hint of doubt about whether this would last. His response was to start turning on our outside lights prior to my daily arrival. Further, honoring him resulted in his coming upstairs to seek me out when he reached a stopping point in his work. Our first interactions went from adversarial to loving. Definitely worth harnessing that difference!

Chapter Seven

Single-Focus: Friend or Foe?

In this chapter, we will examine whether being single-focused in our interactions is a friend or foe. In Gathering Mode, the instinctual point of view is that being of a single-focus mindset separates us. Our goal is to move from Human Raw responses to Human Spirit and create awareness of how we can harness single-focus in such a way that it helps us experience the intangible quality of connection. I understand if that sounds ludicrous at this point. It did for me, too, when I first studied this material.

I need you to draw on your own experiences to begin understanding what I mean when I say that single-focus can be something that separates us. Think of a person or people in your world who, when they have been single-focused on something—whether that is a sport, a hobby, a job, an opportunity, or another person—and their focus has caused you to wonder, *Why would they be so focused on that thing?* Or, possibly, *I just don't get how anyone can see that as being so important.* Can you understand how instinct is already at work as you assume this person or group is misbehaving because their focus is different from yours? In this chapter, we want to unlock some of the misunderstandings that occur around single-focus so we can be empowered to choose our perspective going forward.

If you interact with single-focus out of Human Raw, it will backfire on you and get ugly. For that reason, this chapter will focus on Human Raw and Human Spirit quite a bit.

HUMAN RAW INSTINCTS
TRIGGERED BY SINGLE-FOCUS

In Gathering Mode, the instinct "Am I safe?" shows up very strongly. At this raw, instinctual level, the only way a gatherer can answer yes to this question is when they experience feeling connected. That happening tells gatherers they will be both protected and provided for and, therefore, survive.

In Hunting Mode, instincts show up in two ways. First, as an intense drive to produce a result and, therefore, survive. Second, the subconscious instinctively conceals strengths and weaknesses so the result is not compromised.

Can you see where operating solely out of these conflicting instincts at the Human Raw level does not bode well for relationships? The point of the information in this chapter is to provide a point of view that will equip us to:

- Harness the energy within our instincts.

- Draw on our will, intellect, and emotions to draft responses by:

  ○ Becoming aware of what is possible when we intentionally harness single-focus and put it to good use.

○ Partnering that awareness with the intangible qualities of curiosity, honor, and admiration, thereby creating a result of connection over what is most important to a person.

○ Living from a place of abundance rather than survival.

Are you interested?

OPERATING MODE IMPACTS ON SINGLE-FOCUS

Let's look at three specific attributes of operating modes and how they impact our interactions with single-focus. Those attributes are Focus, Communication, and Safety.

The difference between focus in the two modes is that in Hunting Mode, single-focus instinctively scans out details irrelevant to the current project. In Gathering Mode, diffuse awareness views every single detail as relevant.

Communication in Hunting Mode instinctively conceals both strengths and weaknesses. In Gathering Mode, communication is driven by collecting details—such as how you are like me and how I am like you—so we can connect.

We assess our safety by looking for specific characteristics in the people around us. In Hunting Mode, we look for respect and trust. This tells the hunter they are equipped to produce a result and, therefore, survive. In Gathering Mode, we look for positive attention and interest. This tells a gatherer they are connected and, therefore, will be safe and survive.

It's not hard to see how these three differences could cause unintentional friction in our interactions, is it?

Although both men and women can operate in either mode, we do have defaults because of our levels of testosterone and estrogen. During my research, I asked two different women if they could see how the men in their lives didn't have to deal with diffuse awareness stealing away single-focus. Their responses were:

"I think when I am single-focused,
I am still aware of what I am saying no to in that moment."
–mid-thirties woman

"Makes me mad. My husband can just be single-focused,
and he is not worried about how I feel. How do you do that?"
–mid-sixties woman

In today's world, many women are required to spend large amounts of time in Hunting Mode. This creates neural pathways that become so ingrained that not functioning in Hunting Mode becomes difficult and uncomfortable for some women. Additionally, women's health can be negatively impacted when they live the majority of the time in Hunting Mode. This is because women do not have the natural levels of testosterone required to constantly sustain the intensity of single-focus that is part of Hunting Mode. As a result, women's bodies pull energy from their adrenals, thyroid, liver, and heart to compensate. How many women do you know who have thyroid and adrenal problems?

I'm sharing this mini-biology lesson because when women are equipped with the information in this chapter, they have the opportunity to operate out of both Gathering Mode and Human Spirit, using curiosity to harness single-focus when interacting with others. By living from this perspective, there is no specific result for a woman to produce. It is an opportunity for her to take a break from the demands of Hunting Mode on her body and refuel with great connections!

One last point before we move on to the implementation of this information. In Chapter 5, we reviewed the Center of the Universe (COU) phenomenon, which results from all the details women collect from diffuse awareness. I suggest a quick review of that information before going further in this chapter. COU shows up as a factor in how we express ourselves, both from Human Raw and Human Spirit when interacting with single-focus.

TYPES OF CONVERSATIONS

Our goal is for conversations to be a playground of curiosity. Unfortunately, many times that is not the case when we misunderstand single-focus. Instead, conversations become first-aid stations or interrogation stations.

First aid stations happen when someone in Hunting Mode (male or female) has told a woman about a problem. Women will try to connect by pulling that hunter over into what gatherers would instinctively want—connection via empathy and sharing our feelings. One male research panel member described his experience of being coddled this way:

> "It's like someone is kicking the knees out from underneath me.
> What I really want is just to bounce ideas off."
> –30-year-old male

Do you recall from Chapter 6 that men are natural problem solvers? When a man in Hunting Mode shares a problem, you can connect with him by being curious and asking questions (such as, "Do you want to talk it through with me?" or "What have you come up with as possible solutions?"), then putting on the imaginary duct tape and letting him sort through his thoughts with you.

Interrogation stations happen when someone is in Gathering Mode with instincts directing them. These types of conversations initiate from the mindset that I need "something" from you to be safe and survive. Examples of what that "something" may be are:

- Details that provide certainty, assurance, commitment, or clarification from the person in front of them.

- Details that provide a "hook" into the person in front of them—something they can use to prove their point or manipulate that person. To gain this information, they will use questions like, "Why wouldn't you want to commit to us going out Friday night?"

- Details they can hold against the listener later. These can be attained by the gatherer applying so much pressure that the listener responds with something they don't mean.

Have you guessed that for our conversations to become playgrounds, we need to originate them out of Human Spirit?

Let's look at some distinguishing characteristics of conversations initiated from both Human Raw and Human Spirit when encountering single-focus.

Human Raw Conversations	Human Spirit Conversations
Expects or demands connection. I have to know I have your attention to feel safe.	Uses curiosity to create connection. The initiator is inquisitive about what this single-focus provides for the other person. What excites them about it? Questions help the initiator learn who the person in front of them is—not information about the object of single-focus or how that object relates to the question originator.
Human Raw wants to know how I am like you and how you are like me, so I can know you will protect me. This causes a constant checking of the connection: *Are we connected now? Now? Now?* It is a very surface-level connection.	Because I know who you are, I don't doubt we are still connected, even if your single focus is on something other than me.
Center of the Universe wants to know how this single-focus affects me.	Center of the Universe wants to know what I can contribute. Here's an example: My husband is a studio musician who works out of our home. My part is to give him the time and space he needs to create without interrupting him. When he takes a break, being curious and asking if there is anything he would like me to know about what he is creating offers an opportunity for genuine connection.
Questions are driven by desperation and interrogation.	Questions come from the desire to learn what makes this particular single-focus worth spending time, energy, and money on.
Human Raw perceives single-focus as a threat or enemy.	Human Spirit connects with the person instead of the object of single-focus.

A late-forties male shared an aha moment with me about times he has experienced being threatened by single-focus when his wife, a professional author, is hyper-focused on her writing. He realized that when he chose to support her single-focus, either by sharing in her breakthrough or by offering to brainstorm if she was stuck, he experienced a greater connection with her afterward. He told me, "I love to watch her break through the tough spots when she is writing!"

As part of my research, I asked every male panel member if they would be surprised that many women experience their single-focus as a threat to being able to connect with them. Every one of the men was surprised by this. The consistency of their answer reinforced for me that most men most of the time are not driven by the instinct to connect. My own curiosity was piqued by this, so I asked each male panel member what they wanted women to know about single-focus so they could feel safe. Below are some of their answers:

> "Nine times out of ten, my single-focus is for the betterment of my realm."
> –late-thirties male.

> "Single-focus is like planting a seed that's going to bear the type of fruit that we all want to enjoy later."
> –early-thirties male.

> "I'd like them to realize focus is just focus. It's not something that is meant to insult or alienate anyone else."
> –mid-sixties male

> "Single-focus in no way is a competition."
> –late-sixties male

"I'm not expecting a copy of me."
–mid-twenties male

"If you are patient, you allow us to do single-focus naturally.
Then we can turn our attention to you."
–early-forties male

An important point surfaced during these conversations: Men do not want to be objectified. They don't want to be treated as if they are the thing they are passionate about—that is part of them, but not all of who they are. The bottom line is that being interested in the man personally is much more important to men. My husband said this very succinctly: "You don't have to connect with the 'thing,' just connect with me."

Learning how women can be threatened by single-focus strongly impacted a mid-twenties male research candidate, Jim. I shared with him that before I knew this information about single-focus, I was threatened by my husband's focus on his career to the point I felt I had to compete with it. Jim's immediate response was, "WOW! I never knew women thought that way! I wonder how many women feel threatened by my passion or single-focus."

Jim's concern stemmed from the fact that, at the time of our conversation, he was extremely single-focused on dating! He had been spending a lot of time wondering why dating has to be so hard. *Why can't it be fun and be a thing of honor and respect? Why can't guys treat a woman well without an expectation for a relationship?*

A few days later, Jim told me he had been very busy talking to the women in his circle of friends about how to have a healthy dating culture and make dating fun. He had shifted his single-focus FROM getting a date TO creating a safe, fun environment for both people to share their thoughts on what a first date should be. He'd been asking the women how they would respond to his being authentic if, rather than offering a vague invitation, he were to say, "I would really like to honor you, treat you well, and get to know you better because I think you are awesome. No expectation of anything afterward." It's no surprise that the women responded along the lines of, "This is super helpful!"

The whole point of conversation playgrounds is gaining amazing connections as you learn about the person in front of you. If you choose curiosity, admiration, or honor as the starting point for your communications, I am confident you will discover that what men do externally reflects who they are deep within.

Even after four-plus decades of marriage, I had this experience of discovery with my husband: I came to understand that being a musician is who my husband is, not just what he does.

Being a drummer, he keeps everything about the music steady and creates space for everyone to play well together. I experienced a real aha moment when I recalled his answer to my research question, which asked, "If you had it all your way, what would you provide for those in your realm?" He told me, "The first thing it would be worth it to me to provide would be stability and, after that, a sense of well-being. They would never have to question either one of those concepts." Suddenly, I connected the dots. Keeping things steady and safe for the people around him permeates everything my husband is and does!

THE COST OF BATTLE

Now that we know what single-focus can provide, let's look at what happens when we treat it as a foe and blame it for being the problem in our relationships. I call this the Cost of Battle. I asked two male research panel members, "What capacities do you lose, or who can't you be when you must defend single-focus?" They said:

> "Everybody has to settle for less if single-focus is interrupted and seen as a threat. Then everybody is going to have to settle for a lower quality existence."
> –early-thirties male

> "It's like stealing away a passion."
> –early-twenties male

Additionally, I asked a woman if she had experienced a hunter's single-focus as a threat to their ability to connect. She said:

> "I probably pushed to connect to the point where it [the relationship] broke."
> –late-thirties female

Some tips for starting conversation playgrounds and avoiding the Cost of Battle are:

- Pay attention to how men spend their money, energy, and time. Because men default to single-focus the majority of the time, this tells you what is important to them. Be curious about those things.

- Ask open-ended questions such as "Is there anything you want me to know about {*fill in the blank*}?" These types of inquiries convey respect to anyone in Hunting Mode when their instinct is to conceal information.

- Another reason for open-ended questions is that men are literal. If you ask them a specific question, such as "How was your day?" you will most likely receive a one-word answer, such as "Fine."

- A common breakdown in conversations happens when a male hunter does not ask questions of a female gatherer, thinking he is demonstrating respect. However, the gatherer interprets the lack of questions as the hunter is not interested in them. Gatherers can bridge this gap using questions like "May I tell you about something that makes me happy? I'm passionate about?" The response from the hunter is usually, "Please do!" Or, "I'd love to hear that, but I don't have time right now. Could we talk about this {*day*}?"

- Avoid feigning interest. One male candidate shared with me that a woman had seemed quite interested in his invitation to go to a football game with him. While at the game, it was evident that she did not want to be there. He realized he'd wasted his time, energy, and money because of her feigned interest. The result was his decision not to spend any more time with her. I asked him what would have been a better response and kept the possibility of future interactions open. He said, "If she didn't want to go, just say so!"

CURIOSITY'S TREASURE CHEST

Let's turn our focus to what male hunters experience from playground conversations. I asked my research panel of men, ranging in age from 18 to late 60s, "What does genuine curiosity about your focus and passions provide?"

> "I feel like she is getting into my world. I love that!"
> –early-fifties male

"It's like putting legs on a man to feel stronger and feel supported.
It gets me thinking, *How could I do this for her?*"
–mid-twenties male

"I delight in that space. It's vital to being my best self."
–late-thirties male

"Who doesn't appreciate someone showing interest in them?"
–mid-forties male

"I think it inspires a man to romance."
–late-twenties male

Would access to all of the above and more make it worth consciously using single-focus to connect over what is most important? If so, read on to learn how to partner with and support one another over single-focus.

PARTNERSHIP CHOICES
TO SUPPORT SINGLE-FOCUS

1. I couldn't wait to discuss how to support single-focus with a male candidate on my research panel whose profession is a commercial airline pilot. I was intensely curious to learn how two pilots connect when the job requires such intense focus to provide safety for all aboard.

   His answer was very succinct—Shared Mental Model. This entails three steps. They talk about what they plan to do before doing it. They make sure both people are on the same page with whatever it may be. They come to an agreement, so there are no surprises. We both laughed after this man continued, "You know, that would probably work well for relationships, too, wouldn't it?" I assured him I agreed and would be teaching this!

2. While researching this topic with my husband, I asked him if he had ever been aware that I believed I had to compete with his single-focus on his career—especially while he was a Prince. My question shocked him.

   We had quite a lengthy conversation that helped me see that if I hadn't assumed his focus was something with which I had to compete, I would have been able to see the true motivation for his single-focus. It was and is to be the best version of himself he can be, both for himself and for me. He said, "It's important to understand what is a threat and what isn't."

3. Believing the best of a person is a third way to support single-focus. This was shared with me by the same male panel member who told me that what he wants women to know about single-focus is that, nine times out of ten, his single-focus is for the betterment of his realm.

4. Listen with the sole motivation of learning what something means to the person in front of you. One classmate's research candidate described this experience as "It's intoxicating."

5. Share their interest. This can take many forms: join me, watch me, or let me teach or share with you afterward.

   It deeply moved me when a man in his early thirties described what sharing his passion for writing looked like. He told me he "extended an invitation for relationship" to his four-year-old daughter by sharing his passion for writing and letting her share her passion for creativity. This pushed him to be able to write what she wanted to see. The revelation he had was, "Hey, this is much more fun than writing by myself."

6. Be authentic.

First, I want to speak directly to my female readers about Human Raw instincts impacting the ability to be authentic. Ladies, offering up what you think men want to hear to connect with them is about gaining what you think will keep you safe now. It's exhausting. It will not provide the connection that you want. Instead, it supplies a temporary, desperate, moment-to-moment attachment that constantly needs verifying. An exaggerated example is, "Oh, I'd love to hear you read the Constitution!"

Second, **why would a hunter, whose instinct is to conceal, trust you with their true self if you are not presenting your true self?** You must be willing to be seen for who you truly are in order for hunters to experience the safety they require to let down their guard and allow you to see them. Being authentic like this is how you will find the treasure of real connection. One male research panel member described what he needed to connect this way: "People that are willing to be known and hold space for me to be known."

7. Make choices that empower both people. In my role supporting the CEO, I would love to have an answer as soon as a question arises. Instead, I send my boss—who is only 15 feet away in his office—an email so he can respond when it is a good time for him. That way, we both get what we need. He can maintain his focus without interruption, and I get the information I need.

8. Provide resources that support their single-focus. My brother represented Canada at the World Championship for Curling. He shared with me about the single-focus required to prepare for the moment he had to make the first shot with the Canadian flag on his back. He described the resources of the many individuals who supported him. "People allowed me the time to prepare for that moment in life." I doubt you will be surprised that harnessing his single-focus on this event while using curiosity, admiration, and honor provided an amazing connection and conversation between us!

Providing resources can also include offering the physical resources an individual requires to pursue their focus, such as car rides to a skateboard park or necessary special equipment. One man described resources as everything his many coaches and mentors had poured into his life.

As you consider the point of view you will choose about harnessing single-focus intentionally to connect over what is most important to a person, I leave you with this thought, widely attributed to Walt Whitman: "Be curious, not judgmental."

Chapter 7 - Questions

1. How does single-focus impact women's health? What is the reason for this?

2. What are the three types of conversations? Provide a brief description of each.

3. List three differences between conversations initiated from Human Raw and from Human Spirit.

4. Briefly describe the Cost of Battle. Where have you experienced this in your own life?

5. What three partnership choices would you be willing to make to support single-focus?

6. In your own words, describe why being authentic is so important to successfully supporting single-focus.

REALITY CHECK:

- What surprised you most about what men want women to know about single-focus?

- Where in your life have you experienced a disconnect over single-focus?

Chapter Eight

Piercing Four Seductive Illusions

C an we agree that having the ability to recognize and pierce something deceptive is a good idea? If you concur, keep reading to learn how to harness four seductive illusions at work in all our lives. This chapter also provides an additional tool to improve your life's quality. As you put this into action, the condition of the lives of the people you care about and those you interact with will be impacted for the better.

Let's begin with the definition of "illusion," to be sure we are all at the same starting point.

Illusion: something that deceives
by producing a false or misleading impression of reality.[1]

In Chapter 1, we discussed how we can know we are functioning out of Human Raw instincts by the tension we experience. This is the same for both men and women. Now, we will review four seductive illusions that trigger our instincts, resulting in a perspective of scarcity.

---

1. https://www.dictionary.com/browse/illusion

Our goal is to learn to recognize when our instincts have been triggered and add in our will, intellect, and emotions to create awareness. Next, we aim to partner that awareness with the intangible qualities of freedom, wonder, empowerment, and commitment. This results in us being free to live our lives from a perspective of abundance rather than scarcity.

Let's compare operating out of Human Raw and Human Spirit via this exercise.

Have you experienced at least one incredible, wondrous, abundant moment? For me, this was a bucket list trip my husband and I took, driving the Pacific Coast Highway in a Mustang convertible. I'd like you to think about one of your extraordinary moments. Have you determinedly tried to recreate that moment? Were you successful?

Now close your eyes, take a deep breath, and go to that amazing moment in time. Can you feel it refreshing you? That is the difference between trying to get that wonder back from the scarcity of our own Human Raw efforts versus the abundance we can draw from using Human Spirit. Does living this way interest you?

One male research panel member described living from abundance like this: "It's empowering in a way that makes me want to give myself to the world rather than take life from the world for myself." How would you like to live in a world full of those people?

THE FOUR ILLUSIONS

1. For Women: Happily Ever After / For Men: Life Will Be Better When

These two phrases, "happily ever after" and "life will be better when," are how you can recognize that you or the person speaking are entertaining an illusion.

Some examples are:

I'll *live happily ever after when*...{I marry the right man, accomplish my career goals, find the perfect house, have a child}.

Life will be better when...{I get my MBA, get that promotion, make $$ a year, find the perfect mate}.

2. "The One" (This is the same for women and men.)

"The One" is when we consider that there is one single thing or person out of *all* the options in the universe that will create your happily ever after or make life better. A male research panel member described The One to me this way: "If I can just meet The One person who can see my genius and talent and help me make something of it, then I'll be happy." Can you see scarcity creeping in?

Sometimes, you will hear people use the word "perfect" in conjunction with The One. This not only creates scarcity, but can put The One in the realm of being paralyzing as a person waits for "The One Perfect" opportunity, person, or thing.

3. For Women: Love at First Sight / For Men: Instant Attraction

One man described experiencing instant attraction as "OMG, this might work!" Marketing is all about hopefully creating these responses in both male and female consumers. The goal is to convince possible customers that their product is The One to create happily ever after or make life better by having it.

Women experience love at first sight as a strong connection with someone they don't know or something new to them, such as a house. They quickly become convinced this is The One to create a happily ever after. This constricts their ability to receive input from other people and causes them to live from a scarcity mindset. I will share how this became a problem for one female research candidate when we discuss problems inherent in living from illusions later in this chapter.

4. For Women: It's Meant to Be / For Men: It's Supposed to Be

This fourth illusion, "It's Meant to Be" or "It's Supposed to Be," is the result of the previous three illusions all aligning and coming together. I've listed the four illusions individually below so you can easily see how they flow into one another.

Illusion 4:
Women gather details and men collect facts to create evidence to prove either that this is meant to be or this is supposed to be from
Illusion 3:
the love at first sight/instant attraction for

Illusion 2:

The One thing or person that will provide

Illusion 1:

happily ever after, or will make life better when they have it.

In both genders, the Human Raw instinct is strongly compelled to be right about the fourth illusion. This compulsion becomes a determination to make it happen because all Human Raw sees is the scarcity created by the four illusions. When operating from this instinctual part of our being, the point of view becomes, "It better happen, or I'm going to die!"

An early-fifties male research panel member shared with me how he had been attracted to an opportunity at his company that he initially did not want. This happened because the job was *sold* to him as *The One* thing that would help him advance to the next level in his career and make his life better when he had completed it. That is not what happened. He told me, "The project was supposed to propel my career even further, and it has just stayed the same." Later in this chapter, I will share with you what he told me would have helped him in that situation.

The helpful impact of recognizing and piercing illusions was driven home to me during a research interview with an eighteen-year-old male research panel member. He shared with me how he has always looked to future events to make his life better. His current, specific "life will be better when" was—*if I could only be an adult.* For him, this was *The One* thing that would make the difference he wanted in his life. He was very attracted to the freedom adults have to choose how they spend their time.

I taught him about all four illusions and how they feed one another. Without hesitation, he responded, "I've definitely fallen into the trap of these four illusions!"

The framework of these illusions helped him see the facts he had collected to prove that life would be better when he became an adult. His perception was that the adults around him were free to make decisions when and how they wanted. When he compared that to himself, he felt controlled. He added that our "American Dream" culture constantly sold him on how important it is to be independent and do things how, when, and the way you want.

With his new perspective, he decided to begin immediately working on learning how to make better choices for using his current free time, rather than spending it feeling down and out about the freedoms he currently doesn't have. He's sure that honing that skill will help him make better choices about using his time when he does become an adult. He told me, "I really want to take the time to focus on becoming a better person in the moment rather than look to future events to fix my life."

Are you able to see how illusions can drive your life, taking over your intended place in the driver's seat where you can affect what you want or need to happen?

I asked a late-thirties male research panel member if being aware of these illusions would put him back in the driver's seat. He responded, "Absolutely. You can't get stuck in the future because it doesn't exist, right? The only thing that is real is the present."

So, let's take a look at that driver's seat ...

ATTRIBUTES IDENTIFYING WHO'S IN
THE DRIVER'S SEAT OF OPPORTUNITIES

Before we start driving, play with me here. Please assign one of your hands as Human Raw and the other as Human Spirit. Extend your Human Raw hand as if it were holding a steering wheel. Turn "the wheel" as far as you can in either direction using only that hand. It is limited, correct? Next, switch to your Human Spirit hand to hold and turn the wheel. It uses different muscles, but the results are still limited. Now, use both hands to hold and turn the wheel. Do you see how both hands are needed for the best result? It requires the energy of Human Raw and the awareness and intangible qualities of Human Spirit to create the most abundant outcome.

Lastly, you don't decide to drive with either one or two hands on the wheel for an entire trip—that choice happens moment-to-moment as situations change. With illusions, the amount of energy and awareness required for the best result varies with the circumstances.

The chart on the next two pages identifies attributes a person experiences when operating out of Human Raw or Human Spirit.

	Human Raw Driving Attributes		Human Spirit Driving Attributes
1	**Scarcity.** Scarcity is the result of The One and/or Instant Attraction. A man in his late twenties described the impact of Instant Attraction this way, "It put me in situations where I wouldn't think the whole way through. I spent all my money in high school to get a PlayStation 3. It was not wise."	1	**Abundance.** Operating out of abundance means being aware that you don't know what you don't know. One man described living from the perspective of abundance as: "It doesn't hurt to try on a few pairs of shoes before you see which one fits."
2	**Fear/Tension.** I asked a female research panel member if she'd experienced fear and tension caused by an opportunity morphing into a threat in her thoughts. She said, "I think as an artist that feeling always lives with me. It always feels vulnerable to share my paintings or writing."	2	**Freedom/Wonder.** The good news is, once aware of this information, the same woman made choices to live from Human Spirit. She's now experiencing the freedom and wonder of pursuing her creativity from the abundance of having a mentor, an entrepreneurial advisor, and creative friends who know she values their input.
3	**Am I safe?** Though we crave safety, it can be argued that being safe does not equal being fulfilled. I asked my brother, whose career is in education, if he ever experienced an abundance of opportunities. He shared that he once had several job offers and was being chased and pressured to move into education administration. Administration would provide immediate safety with more financial and prestige rewards; however, it would also remove the satisfaction and enjoyment he experienced in the classroom and coaching.	3	**Am I empowered?** After considering his options, my brother empowered himself by staying in the classroom and experiencing satisfaction and enjoyment until he retired. To this day, he continues to teach coaches how to coach.

	Human Raw Driving Attributes		Human Spirit Driving Attributes
4	**Succeed = Survive; Fail = Die** Human Raw functions with a scarcity mindset, which perpetuates decisions being very black/white, right/wrong. It perceives only one way to do something. This triggers our instincts, compelling us to take action out of desperation, using the measurement of success = survival and failure = die.	4	**Options to be explored.** Human Spirit does not limit our options. A male research panel member in his mid-thirties shared he had spent four years in a job that was not exciting to him but "paid the bills." Rather than perceiving he had to succeed in that job to survive, he researched opportunities, met with multiple people, and carefully explored and planned options with many parties. The result was that he formed a new company, tendered his resignation at his old company, and recently told me he now has four full-time employees working for him.
5	**Determined.** Being determined shows up as a "get 'er done" attitude—when we do whatever it takes to ensure that what happens is what we believe is supposed to be or meant to be. Why? Because Human Raw discerns that something must be right and successful for us to survive.	5	**Committed.** Commitment is to pledge to or engage in the pursuit of a goal. This is done from an open mindset of being creative and willing to explore how to achieve that goal.

Does being aware of these attributes help you see where Human Raw or Human Spirit has been in the driver's seat of opportunities in your life or those around you? It did me.

I started my certification journey from Human Spirit to help men and women better understand each other. I committed myself to the freedom of living from the joy and wonder of this adventure. I wanted to discover the abundance of all the possibilities of who I might become and the impact that might have on the lives around me. However, I was unaware that even as the course progressed, I was exchanging freedom, joy, and wonder for tension, fear, frustration, and dogged determination so I could reach my goal perfectly—until I learned about the four illusions.

While listening to one of my instructors, I learned a definitive way to determine if you are operating out of Human Raw or Human Spirit. Ask: Does the opportunity present itself as "a new standard of perfection" or "an opportunity to be empowered"?

Ding! Ding! Ding! The light bulb went on for me! Perfection had become my "One Thing" that would provide my happily ever after. I researched harder and taught more, determined to make perfection happen. Talk about an illusion!

The abundance, joy, wonder, and freedom of this opportunity had been replaced by "buckle down and get 'er done so I could succeed = survive."

Am I able to say I'm no longer vulnerable to being seduced by the illusion of perfection? No. However, being aware of this illusion helps me notice fear, tension, and dogged determination as "red flags" notifying me who is driving my opportunity. Noticing empowers me to choose to stop, take a deep breath, and switch drivers!

FOUR PREVALENT PROBLEMS
WHEN LIVING OUT OF ILLUSIONS

We run into problems when we believe the illusions. The first problem is squinting, which directly results from Human Raw's determination. We squint, adjusting our perception so that what we see lines up with our goal, proving the illusion is what it is meant to be or is supposed to be. Love at first sight became a problem for a late-thirties female research panel member. I asked if she had ever been so sure of The One that she became determined to make it happen. She said, "I was so convinced he was 'the person' for me, I really did turn inside in terms of not wanting to hear other people's concerns or doubts."

An early-thirties male on my research panel shared that squinting caused a close call regarding a job opportunity. He thought this opportunity was The One due to instant attraction. The way he explained the situation, in considering this opportunity, he distorted everything about the company that didn't fit with his ethics. Fortunately, he and his wife always consult one another before making big decisions, and together, they uncovered the illusion. He shared that he is so very thankful he did not pursue the job, as the business is now literally falling apart.

The second problem stems from differences in how women and men view problems associated with an opportunity. Do you recall from Chapter 6 how women are uncomfortable with the word "problem"? Discomfort leads women to believe that if problems occur around an opportunity, then obviously, it is NOT meant to be—"It's just too hard." Ladies, would it surprise you to learn that men actually *expect* solving problems to be part of an opportunity? What men don't expect are insurmountable problems.

These two points of view can cause a real disconnect when a man is pursuing an ambition (not an illusion), and a woman's illusion is that it's not "meant to be" because there are problems to be solved.

The third problem with illusions is that sometimes "meant to be" doesn't happen.

While researching with a male panel member who is an Elder (refer back to Chapter 4) about "meant to be" not happening, he told me, "Retirement was supposed to be the golden years, and at the moment, it is the hobbled years." I asked him how he and his wife dealt with that. He said, "Come up with new goals to accomplish, things to look forward to, and release what life tried to sell you would happen."

The fourth and biggest problem with illusions is blind spots. This problem is large enough to warrant its own section.

BLIND SPOTS

Think of when you have been driving and could not see something without help or changing your viewing position. I asked a late-sixties panel member if he would approach another man about a blind spot and, if so, how he would do it. He answered, "Isn't that what the golf course is for? Or fishing? Do something you enjoy, then bring up the awkward stuff."

When I asked a mid-fifties panel member to provide his advice about pointing out blind spots, he started with what NOT to do. He had three points:

- DON'T tell someone else *what to do.*

- DON'T say, "That's crazy."

- DON'T say, "Can I tell you why that is a horrible idea?" (Yes, several people had literally said this to him!)

Multiple male research panel members told me that to point out a blind spot to someone successfully, you must have a relationship with them. One man put it this way: "It needs to come from CONNECTION, NOT CORRECTION. If you just come to CORRECT without CONNECT, then you don't have any credibility with me, and we are just fighting."

All twelve members of my research panel for this topic told me that what would work best for someone to approach them about a blind spot is some form of **questions that direct them to what they are not thinking about**. Before I provide a list of the specific questions they suggested, please always remember to ask these questions with curiosity from Human Spirit. Do not initiate these questions from Human Raw, as it would come across as an interrogation.

The list below is eight responses to the question, "What is the best thing someone could say to help you see a blind spot?"

1. "Are you sure about this?"

2. "You might want to rethink that."

3. "Did you consider _____?"

4. "Will this support who you truly are?"

   ○ This question came from the man who was squinting about the job opportunity.

5. "Could this backfire on you?"

   ○ This question came from the man who was "sold" on taking a job he didn't want, believing it would improve his life once he completed it. He explained he never considered that the opportunity could backfire. If someone had asked him, "Could this backfire?" he would have had a Plan B.

6. Ask someone to reverse-engineer the situation.

   ○ For example: "OK, say you get the new car and bigger monthly payment, then what?"

7. "Can I call a Safe Zone?"

   ○ This is a literal deal a husband and wife created, which occurs when one of them calls a time-out and asks, "Can you listen, not defend yourself, and just hear me right now?"

8. "May I share from my experience what I learned when faced with this situation?"

When engaging in this manner, it's essential to grant your listener the freedom to respond contrary to what you had hoped. Even when they do, your question will likely cause them to relook at their situation privately.

A late-twenties male panel member summed up discussing blind spots this way: "The goal is not to change someone, but to plant seeds that will grow and almost feel like it's their idea."

SEVEN PARTNERSHIP CHOICES SURROUNDING ILLUSIONS AND BLIND SPOTS

Conversations about helping each other recognize illusions and see our blind spots are very sensitive. Because these interactions are piercing and may burst the bubble of a person's illusion, they must be initiated by Human Spirit.

The first choice must be to **have your partner's back,** no matter what. A mid-sixties male panel member put it this way: "The best way to get these opportunities to maybe help a person see a blind spot is to support the person regardless of their choice."

Second, **exercise respect**. We have discussed the importance of respecting those in Hunting Mode to ensure they experience safety. Some ways to demonstrate respect are:

- If the person in Hunting Mode is male, respect the stage of development that is driving and compelling them.

- Respect that honor—being true to self—is behind male etiquette, team, and competition.

- Respect the time and energy both male and female hunters put into creating and executing their plans.

Third, **assume the best** of the person in front of you. Men have brought up this action as a way to be supported in every topic in this book. This is where we started building our foundation with the three questions: *What if no one is misbehaving? What if there is a good reason for that? What if we are misunderstanding?*

Fourth, **exercise kindness**. A mid-twenties male panel member told me it's quite possible he could initially get upset if someone asked him about a possible blind spot. However, if they "killed him with kindness," this would quickly turn him to thinking, *Dang it, I am doing that; I do need to think about that.*

Fifth, **be courageous**. A mid-thirties woman shared with me about a blind spot she can now see that she had when she was younger. She believed "doing it on her own" was The One way for her success to be real. I asked her what might have helped her to see that sooner. She said, "I'm wondering if it would have taken equal parts of someone being willing to get in my face about it, but also hearing it from someone who wasn't expecting anything of me."

Sixth, **exercise curiosity and interest**. Listen and watch to learn about the person in front of you rather than the thing being discussed. You can refer to Chapter 7 about harnessing single-focus for more details. If you notice something that may be one of these illusions or a blind spot, use any of the eight questions listed above to help point their thinking toward what they might not be seeing.

Seventh, **speak directly to the point or problem**. These conversations are not the time to discuss details. Again, employ the eight questions listed in this chapter to discuss blind spots.

I have one last quote from a forty-year-old Middle Prince about these four illusions. He compared living in illusions to a silver bullet—a simple and seemingly magical solution to a complicated problem. His quote is long but worth reading.

> "Silver bullets don't exist, and if they did,
> we wouldn't shoot them because they'd be too
> expensive. If you're waiting for a silver bullet,
> [know that] even if you had it, you
> wouldn't be good enough to hit the target because
> you never practiced shooting at that target.
>
> I learned the lesson that silver bullets are a
> farce and a fairy tale. You hit the target by

practice and consistently shooting at the target.
You miss a lot of times, but you eventually get good
at hitting that target. For me, it is not consistency;
it's persistence and practice in a single direction.
It's having a focus and knowing what you are going after. I
don't look for silver bullets to get me anywhere.
I just look for my own commitment to
something, my own innovation, and my own creativity."

It's your choice what point of view you will have about these illusions. You decide whether you will live in the scarcity they create or pierce them so you can live in the abundance of unknown possibilities. That choice is yours with each opportunity.

Chapter 8 - Questions

1. List the four seductive illusions and describe each in your own words.

2. In your own words, describe how illusions drive our lives.

3. Compare two attributes of Human Raw vs. Human Spirit being in the driver's seat.

4. What are the four problems prevalent with illusions?

5. Do you resonate with any of the questions to help recognize blind spots? Which ones? Are you willing to share those questions with people who influence your life?

6. What partnership choice to pierce illusions or blind spots would be most difficult for you? Do you see value in dismantling this discomfort to partner with those important to you?

REALITY CHECK:

- How have you been influenced by these illusions in your life?

- Has there been a time someone tried to point out a blind spot to you? How did you react? What would have helped you?

Chapter Nine

Creating Connection through Competition and Ambition

W hen my instructor introduced me to the idea that competition and ambition can create connection, I was substantially skeptical. Picture a large question mark hanging over my thoughts. In what world could a matchup bring people together? Imagine my surprise when I discovered that world was mine!

To bring us to the same starting point for this chapter, please refer to Chapter 2, Stumbling Block #4, to refresh yourself on the different Human Raw perspectives of competition in men and women.

In this chapter, we will delve deeper to uncover what's possible when we harness the energy of competition and ambition by supporting both. For estrogen-based readers, you may wonder *why* a person would even want to do this. I'll cut to the chase. It helps you and the people around you be the best version of themselves. Sound worth it?

To discover a point of view that will help you harness the primal energy of competition and ambition, we begin by adding our intellect, emotions, and will to form a response consisting of an awareness of what competition can provide and what's possible when we mix in the intangible qualities of listening, curiosity, and support. This process equips us to experience the result of living from the abundance of being our best selves and winning the pursuit of our Dearest Goals and Heart's Desires.

A necessary tool for success in this area is Listening to Learn, which we discussed in Chapter 1, Essential #5.

While researching this topic with my husband, I employed Listening to Learn when I asked him how he wins during our interactions. He was quiet as he thought about his response and then said, "Am I competing to make you laugh? Hell yes! Am I competing to make you like me? Love me? Want me? Desire me? *Absolutely*, because there is somebody else out there who might want to do the same, and you might look at them more than you look at me." His response literally took my breath away. At the time, we'd been married forty-three years, and he still competes for me to choose him every day. Now, I am aware of his mindset, and I continually see this in how he treats me. What a gift!

MALE AND FEMALE
COMPETITIVE PRIMAL ENERGY VIEWPOINTS

How primal is competition in males? In Chapter 2, we pointed out that competition begins at the cellular level and is encoded in the male's DNA. However, females can definitely choose from Human Spirit to engage with competition the way men default to it.

Competition in the youngest of men is easy to see. One male research panel member told me about his two and three-year-old sons. He said, "My two sons are constantly competing with each other. I don't think I taught them that. I think they just are that way."

At the Human Raw level for women, our instincts tell us that connection equals safety. This means *anything* that appears to get in the way of connection, including competition and ambition, causes us to feel threatened and unsafe.

The answers to the five questions below are initiated from the Human Raw level for most men most of the time and most women most of the time. FYI–each answer from men is followed by a specific quote from a male research panel member for the benefit of my female readers—to help them know I'm not making this up!

Question #1—What does competitive mean?
Men: A way to put best beside best to grow and improve.
Quote: "Being competitive is doing your best." –late sixties male
Women: Competition is childish and immature. Men should just grow up and get over it.

Question #2—How do you describe competition?
Men: It's fun!
Quote: "They push you; you push back. You keep giving each other energy." –early-teens male
Women: Women get angry because they believe they can't win when they compete. They may be rejected for winning and viewed as insufficient or even be rejected for losing.

Question #3—Do men compete with themselves? Others?
Men: Both. Most men believe competition strengthens a team.
Quote: "All of the above. It's not the 'I'm better than you'

thing. It's 'let's be as good as WE can be.'" –early-fifties male
Women: Women believe competition can destroy relationships.

Question #4—What is your viewpoint about competition?
Men: Most men are grateful for competition.
Quote: "We clash because we care. We're going to figure it
out. If I don't express my opinion, I'm not doing my job."
–late-fifties male, a senior manager, about his co-workers
Women: Rather than gratitude, most women experience
angst and upset. You may hear them say, "Why can't we all
just get along?"

Question #5—Do you think about honor and competition
very much?
Men: Most believe competition is honorable and approach it
from that perspective.
Quote: "I think about both pretty much constantly. If you
win the competition without being honorable, it's a pretty
hollow win." –mid-sixties male
Women: Women can reach a point of hatred for competition
because they believe they cannot win, think it will destroy
connections with others, and competition causes them so
much angst.

The bottom line is that when men and women approach competition
from the Human Raw portion of our makeup, we are pretty much polar
opposites. This is very fertile ground for misunderstanding to take root
and grow.

As I mentioned in Chapter 1, Stumbling Block #4, there is one caveat. Women are being taught at younger and younger ages to engage in competitive sports, which teaches them skills to be comfortable with competition. However, their instinctual responses may still show up depending on the circumstances.

WHAT MEN WANT WOMEN TO KNOW ABOUT AMBITION AND COMPETITION

I asked every male research panel member, "If you could tell women anything about ambition and competition, what would you want us to know?" Here are some answers I received.

> "Ambition and competition are not the same as recklessness."
> –early-thirties male

This man seemed to want to say more, so I put on my imaginary duct tape and waited. He continued by telling me he really would like to know what would help his wife trust his ambition and competitiveness. His reason was, "By that trust, I feel equipped to use the ambition and competition to make our life as a family more rich and wonderful."

> "Manage your emotions when it comes to competitiveness."
> –early-fifties male

> "Men need to see things hang in the balance and for us to pull it off."
> –late-fifties male

This response made me very curious, so I asked this follow-up question: "What part of themselves do men lose if they can't compete?" He responded, "We lose our dreams. We disconnect, and we just quit playing the game."

> "Competition is motivation."
> –fourteen-year-old male

> "I'm not upset. I'm just passionate."
> –mid-twenties male

> "Competition and ambition are healthy
> on both sides of the table."
> –late-thirties male

This man elaborated on his comment, stating that he believes competition is a good thing for both females and males.

> "Men are genuinely better people
> when they have good cheerleaders."
> –forty-year-old male

I again applied my imaginary duct tape and waited after this comment. He explained that seeing his wife as a cheerleader was not an objectification. Rather, he sees her as a powerful partner. He said, "My wife is my biggest cheerleader, and I'm a better man for it."

Take a moment to digest these panel-member remarks. **Can you observe how, when women—myself included—try to keep both ourselves and the men in our lives "safe" from competition and ambition, we kill the very life, romance, and adventure we want to flourish?** Do you see how supporting competition and ambition could be a good thing?

A GLIMPSE INTO AMBITION LANE

By this point in my research, I was fascinated by the consistency of men equating ambition and competition with being their best. I started asking them, "What do you want to be the best at?"

> "I decided a long time ago I was going to be a better
> husband and father than anything else."
> –forty-year-old male

> "Competition and ambition make us a
> better person for someone else."
> –mid-sixties male

> "The thing I want to be best at is
> I want to be the best version of me."
> –late-fifties male

I used my imaginary duct tape to find out if he would share what that might be. He continued, "The best version of me is being the best at loving my wife, my kids, and my grandkids."

If you are wondering how to know if what a man is sharing with you is an ambition or just something he is daydreaming about, look for whether he is expending energy on that thing. A late-thirties male told me, "It's just a daydream unless you do something about it."

One of my female clients shared how this information about ambition impacted her. Previously, Ellen had only seen disconnection when she disagreed with what a man was sharing with her. The bigger the disagreement, the more disconnection she felt.

Recently, she started to date someone new. Shortly before Ellen took this class, they discovered a topic they adamantly disagreed on. I taught her the principle of Listening to Learn. We discussed that for most men most of the time, ambitions center around being the best version of themselves because of what that provides for the people they care about.

After the class, Ellen went on another date with this man and continued their conversation. Ellen was able to shift her listening point of view. She let go of the disconnection because of their disagreement and heard why this man was so passionate about his beliefs. She learned the fervor behind his ambition came from his drive to be an incredible provider—not just now but for his future family. Everything he told her was tied to that ambition. She realized the disagreement wasn't about her, her beliefs, or an attack. Her new listening perspective allowed them to discuss how they would navigate this topic if their relationship progressed.

Ellen told me, "I realized he wasn't trying to change my mind, but rather he was letting me in on something very important to him. It's part of what he wants to do and who he wants to be."

Passion is not the only thing that can drive ambition. Wounds can also initiate it. A mid-fifties male panel member shared how he made a huge career change in his mid-forties. He looked at his life and realized he didn't want to invest the remainder of his life in the finance career he had established. He was successful, but that path was pushed upon him when he was young. I asked him how ambition showed up before and after that change. He said, "The ambition behind my business career was to provide something, and the fear of losing everything. My ambition now is, indeed, to be someone."

WHOSE AMBITION IS IT?

We need to examine what happens when it is unclear whose ambition is being sought after. I asked an early-sixties female research panel member, "What made you think a man should be engaged in an activity he wasn't?" She answered, "It was my expectation. It was important to me. Why wasn't it important to him?" The problem was that she had not communicated how important this activity was to her. Her *expectation* was that he should just know.

What's at the root of this misunderstanding? The difference between diffuse awareness and single-focus. First, do you see how someone with diffuse awareness, which causes every detail to be important, could have the expectation that everyone else is collecting every detail about her and, therefore, *should* know what is and isn't important to her? Second, imagine this expectation intersecting with a person in Hunting Mode who is only collecting details relevant to the current goal. It is not surprising that friction is the result.

I asked a mid-thirties woman, "Have you ever decided what someone else should be ambitious about?" She answered, "I have trouble separating potential from what they actually want." As we continued our conversation, she shared that pushing a man to be ambitious where *she* saw potential became part of what drove them apart. She told me he said, "It's just one more way I can't make you happy."

One final piece that supports the importance of knowing who the ambition originates from relates to what we learned about The Plan in Chapter 5: Hunters commit to The Plan, which is made up of the hunter's strengths, resources, and values, and avoids their weaknesses. *Nowhere* in The Plan is what someone else sees as the hunter's potential taken into account.

COMPETITION—WHO AND WHEN?

Getting right to the point of who the competition involves and when it occurs, the answers are: the man in the mirror and 24/7.

I'm a little slow. I never understood that men literally compete with the man in the mirror. Even when they compete with another person, they still compete with themselves to be and do their best. One mid-twenties research panel member told me about being the best: "I'm OK not being #1, as long as we are doing our best."

My husband described competing with the man in the mirror this way: "When people are competing against themselves, they are competing against doubt. We have to compete with that doubt to overcome it."

I asked a fourteen-year-old male research panel member what he needed in place to put forth his best effort. He said, "I just always wanna do the best I can, always compete with everybody."

I asked a man in his late thirties if he competes with himself as well as others. He told me, "I would say I compete with myself almost exclusively."

A man in his mid-twenties told me the purpose of competing is "to be a steward of excellence."

I asked a man in his sixties if he was aware of always competing. He said, "I feel like I always, or most of the time, am competing about something or with something."

I asked a forty-year-old male research panel member if anything is still worth doing when you are not the best. He said, "Fatherhood comes to mind. Husbandry. Love in general. Compassion. Kindness. I'm not going to be great at those things, but they are definitely worth doing."

Are you starting to grasp what's possible to discover when you use Listening to Learn?

Have you noticed that none of the men indicated they were aiming for perfection? They aim to be "a better man." Compare that to how many times you've heard a woman use the word perfect to describe her goals about herself or a project. At an instinctual level, women believe perfection is necessary to experience the connection they long for to feel safe. Female instincts quickly tell women, *If you're not perfect, you will be rejected.* Having this mindset causes women to be very hard on themselves. It makes us feel defeated and defensive. Perhaps we could take a tip from the men around us and try to be *better* women rather than *perfect* women. What if we extend that to our goals of being a better partner, a better boss or co-worker, a better friend, a better parent, being better at exercise and health choices, and having our homes look better? Being *better* is achievable. Being perfect is not. Let's exchange our goals by being kind to ourselves and striving to grow better rather than demanding perfection.

WHAT'S A WIN?

Winning is definitely a part of ambition and competition, but what exactly is a win? As I researched, I discovered this acronym, popularized by former Notre Dame football coach Lou Holtz.

What's
Important
Now

The above phrase succinctly summarizes what men were telling me: the definition of winning is not static.

> "It's always a gauge. Is my energy, effort, and time
> worth what I'm going to get out of this?"
> –early-fifties male

> "Anything that gets me closer to a goal
> or a win is a win in itself."
> –late-fifties male

I also learned that part of a win is found in pursuing a goal. Hunters experience an incredible peace that is part of being completely immersed in their focus on the goal. My husband described it this way:

> "Every guy wants to be overtaken by the essence
> of what he wants to do—
> at that point, it's just pure freakin' bliss."

A fourteen-year-old male research panel member provided a metaphor to describe this peace.

> "It's not like you start something, and you are
> instantly at peace. It's like someone who is afraid
> of flying getting on a plane.
> They are afraid at the beginning,
> but once you get into the air,
> it's just kinda peaceful.
> You barely notice you're in the air
> if you don't look outside."

In comparison, gatherers experience that beautiful peace in quite a different way. In Chapter 1, we discussed that what makes something Worth-It for gatherers is being able to check off their objective(s) when completed.

For this reason, once a goal is on their horizon, there can be no peace until that goal is reached. Being able to putter/dawdle/tinker freely with no goal to be accomplished is when gatherers experience that wonderful, encompassing peace.

REFUELING BY REFRAMING

All this ambition, competition, and winning takes energy. Imagine a glass half-empty. Refueling by reframing is imagining that same glass as being half-full. I discovered that reframing provides renewed access to primal competitive energy, which empowers hunters with the viewpoint that they have what they need to succeed = survive. Pretty important and very energizing! Every panel member I asked about this phenomenon told me it happens without thinking about it.

I asked multiple male research panel members to share their personal experiences of refueling by reframing a win. Even though their experiences were very unique, their overall result was the same.

> "It's the re-ignition of your focus."
> –mid-fifties male senior executive

> "What looked like winning yesterday looks
> like losing today. You've got to adapt."
> –forty-year-old father

The man who provided the quote above was referencing raising his children. When they were younger, it felt like a win to him to exercise enough control to make sure his children made safe choices. As they got older, control did not work, and he had to redefine winning. Winning became giving them space to experience life while maintaining connection.

My fourteen-year-old great-nephew runs cross country. He described re-framing as "that one little switch in your brain." He shared that when he is in the middle of the pack, rather than having to beat everyone, he tells himself:

> "It's just one guy. I can make this little push."

My husband's description of reframing is:

> "You refresh yourself in the thought,
> *I don't have to do as much*
> *as I thought I was going to have to do.*"

His response made me curious, so I asked this follow-up question: "Are you accessing new energy?"

> "It is not necessarily new energy.
> Rather, reframing makes your reserves seem bigger."

My final reframing example comes from my brother, who has competed at the World Championship for Curling four times, representing Canada. He won silver as a coach in 2002, gold as an athlete in 2003, bronze as an athlete in 2004, and fifth place as an athlete in 2005. He shared with me that thousands of people began training with the goal of winning the gold medal, himself included. Even when he didn't win the gold but earned another color medal, he still considered himself to have won, knowing so many others didn't make it to the podium at all. He told me:

> "I still think winning the silver medal
> is not losing."

DEAREST GOALS

Why is supporting ambition and competition so important? You help set people on the path to win at their Dearest Goal and Heart's Desires. First, we will examine Dearest Goals.

When initiated by Human Spirit, a person's Dearest Goals are driven by their passions. The goal is an expression of who they are. Achieving a Dearest Goal is both fulfilling and energizing. A woman on my research panel shared that her Dearest Goal to be a medical missions nurse in Africa began when she was a teenager. Twenty years later, she achieved that goal for the first time. She has done it every year since. She said:

> "To be able to finally get to that goal line
> and cross over was very fulfilling
> and life-changing."

A single man in his mid-twenties expressed his Dearest Goal this way:

> "I really want to father—
> being a husband and loving someone super well.
> Then, being a father, loving that child super well, and
> seeing them be successful."

In contrast, some goals originate from Human Raw. These goals show up where a wound has hijacked a person's life with an endless longing to fill an insatiable need. A male research panel member in his mid-sixties described this kind of goal as:

> "It's not even a temporary gain,
> it's just more of a frustration of,
> *I've got to do this again now.*"

You can recognize goals derived from wounds because they are draining rather than energizing. They have the quality of, *It's never enough, no matter what is achieved*. If you do notice goals driven by wounds when you are Listening to Learn, you can support the person by using kindness and curiosity to ask *one* of these questions:

- Why is this important to you?

- What are you gaining from this?

Then, put on your imaginary duct tape and listen. The questions above help a person see themselves. Depending on your relationship with the individual, you may be able to suggest a healing modality.

HEART'S DESIRES

Heart's Desires are distinguished from Dearest Goals by being circumstance-specific rather than an expression of who a person is. They require courage and vulnerability to uncover and partnership with others to achieve. A Heart's Desire can be for the next four hours, the next day, your next vacation, your next career move, or even your next life goal. They have two unique parts—WHAT and HOW.

The **WHAT Finder Tool** is this question: *In this circumstance, if you had it all your way and did not have to justify it to anyone or deserve it, WHAT would you do?*

I asked a male research panel member in his late thirties, who had recently started his own business, WHAT his Heart's Desire was. He told me he thought he might be living it! He said,

"I can see the success in the way that I
thought it might be able to be possible.
I can see that in the path ahead of me."

It's time for an exercise to help convey the interaction of a WHAT and the HOW Monster.

Pick one of your hands—it doesn't matter which one. Hold this hand out in front of you as if you are receiving a gift. This is your WHAT holder hand. Take your other hand and hold it out to your side like a police officer holding up their hand to stop traffic. The traffic being stopped is the HOW Monster. It is amazing how quickly this monster shows up to squash a newborn WHAT.

But what if you permitted someone you trust to be your HOW Monster Police, rather than you having to do both things? This is partnership in its simplest form. It sets people up to win at their Dearest Goals and Heart's Desires. In our example, entrusting someone to be your HOW Monster Police enables you to use both your hands to hold your WHAT, examine it, and define it using your imagination and ambition. You can allow your WHAT to grow and become more beautiful.

The person acting as your HOW Monster Police has the opportunity to think of possible hows or who might know how. Can you see that both your WHAT and HOW can grow exponentially because of your partnership?

I've pretty much been a victim of the HOW Monster my entire life, up to a few years ago. It was too scary to invest the time and energy to figure out my Heart's Desire, let alone speak it out. I realize now that it was easier to blame someone for my unhappiness rather than figure out what truly would make me happy and own that.

However, the more my life was transformed by the material I was studying about understanding men and women, the more a dream started to pop up. It was quickly squashed by the HOW Monster, pointing out the cost, the time required, and my age.

As I learned about discovering the WHAT of my Heart's Desire, I also learned what sharing my Heart's Desire with my husband provided for him. It allowed him to help make my dream come true and be my hero. Both of these things are ambitions he always has.

Now, I KNOW that finding and speaking Heart's Desires changes lives.

I remember sitting across from my husband at Jason's Deli restaurant, sharing this crazy idea that, rather than taking more individual courses to help me, maybe I should pursue being certified to train and coach other people. I could help transform lives and marriages the way we had been helped. I told him I hadn't felt this passionate about anything in a very long time. I can still feel my nervousness as I shared how expensive it would be and how much time it would require. I was completely undone as he looked me in the eyes, agreed he thought this was the best plan of action, and encouraged me to find out more about it.

That led to me applying and being accepted. Suddenly, my Heart's Desire was about to become real. My response? *OH MY GOSH, what have I done? HOW will I do this?*

I shared my fear of the HOW with my husband. At that moment, he became and remained throughout the process my HOW Police to protect me. He told me, "I don't have to believe in your mentor. I don't have to believe in the organization. I believe in you."

PARTNERSHIP CHOICES

We need to look at a new tool to facilitate strong partnerships. It's called A Great Ask. I bring it up here because partnership is integral to someone achieving their Heart's Desires. However, A Great Ask can be employed anywhere in your life when you partner with another person.

The components of A Great Ask are:

Step 1: State your need without any "because."

- If you are asking on your behalf, say, "I need _____."

- To find out what support someone else needs, ask, "What support do you need?"

Step 2: A description of what is needed.

- If you are asking on your behalf, "This need met would look like _____." Include what it would look like, not look like, when you need it, or how often.

- If you are asking about providing support to someone else, ask, "What does this support look like to you? When do you need it? How often?"

Step 3: A description of what receiving the fulfillment of this need would provide.

- "This need met would provide _____." Include what you could be, do, have room for, think, feel, or experience in life if you received this supply.

- If asking someone else about supporting them, ask, "What would this support provide for you?"

When asking on your own behalf, be sure to close by asking the other person, "What do you need to give me what I'm asking you for?" This helps the person you are asking take stock of their own needs and their ability and willingness to provide for your need.

If you are the one providing support to someone else, check with yourself whether there is anything you require from the person needing your support to make it possible or make you want to provide for them. Share what you need to be able to or want to assist them. Examples could be appreciation or a different time frame.

In line with the principles of A Great Ask, I asked the members of my research panel what support to pursue their Dearest Goals and Heart's Desires would look like to them. Think about it—what would the world be like if we lived from this place?

"Give me time when I need it. That's the best gift."
–late-sixties male

"Providing resources."
–multiple panel members

Examples of the resources referenced by panel members included mentoring, networking, time, money, effort, help to secure grants, words of affirmation, sports equipment, and transportation to games.

"Patience."
–early-fifties male

This man invests a lot of time and energy in his job. He needs the patience of his family to know he is doing this to make their lives better.

"Believe the best of me even
if I'm not being the best version of me."
–forty-year-old male

This man told me that when his family believes in him, it helps him return to being his best self.

"'That's a good idea.'"
–late-fifties male

This male panel member shared that hearing this phrase affirms and encourages him. It tells him he has been heard and understood.

"Motivation."
–fourteen-year-old male

This young man described motivation as someone pushing you towards a goal you have indicated that you want to achieve.

"Genuine interest in the person."
–mid-twenties male

This male research participant elaborated: be interested in the person and encourage them, even if you don't share the same passion for the goal. He stressed being both kind and *authentic*. Female instincts can work against authenticity to guard against relational disconnect. You can recognize this when women say things like "Of course, you can do that" when they don't believe it. The ground under both people crumbles if the goal is not reached. Acting this way is the opposite of the next point.

"Masculine kindness."
–mid-sixties male

Masculine kindness may not necessarily feel like kindness at first. It is authentic support from a respected source who recognizes that the individual's continued investment of time, energy, and money in a particular goal is a waste. An example comes from my brother, who taught high school physics for many years.

> "I have had students... [for whom] science
> has been a foreign language...
> They have told me they are going to be doctors.
> I have had discussions [telling them]
> they should investigate how much science
> is involved with being doctors.
> If they really, truly dislike science,
> [they should] re-evaluate...being a doctor."

Before you decide on your perspective for supporting competition and ambition to help bring out the best in all of us as we pursue our Dearest Goals and Heart's Desires, I have one last quote for you. This was shared with me from a man who wanted women to see that competition, ambition, and all the things that go with them are necessary. He *really* wanted women not to feel disconnected, hurt, or put off by a man trying to make his way through the world doing these things, because that is just who men are. He concluded by saying:

> "It's best to accept and see that a man
> needs to do this not only for himself but for you,
> to accomplish the goals he wants for you;
> to be better for you; to make you feel he's worthy.
> I think every man wants to feel like what they're doing
> is helping the woman to choose him."
> –sixty-five-year-old Elder

Chapter 9 - Questions

1. What surprised you most about how men and women view competition from a Human Raw Perspective?

2. Why is it important to be clear on whose ambition it is?

3. What is refueling by reframing? Have you experienced this in your own life or seen it in the lives around you?

4. Describe what a Dearest Goal is. What Dearest Goal do you have?

5. Describe what distinguishes a Heart's Desire from a Dearest Goal.

6. What are the components of A Great Ask?

REALITY CHECK:

- In what three places in your life would A Great Ask help you achieve better results, either to get the help you need or to support someone else?

- Write out a list of Heart's Desires you have. Next to each one, list a person with whom you could partner to be your HOW Monster police.

Epilogue

Despite everything I have and continue to learn, my husband and I still bump into one another's instincts and misunderstand each other from time to time. If this happens to you after you put all you have read into action, please don't let it cause you to give up. Now, when something goes awry, I quickly recognize that I must be missing something. Experience has taught me that the wisest choice I can make in these situations is to take time to reflect.

The enlightenment that comes amazes me. When I consciously interact by harnessing my instincts with my will, intellect, and emotions, it creates space within my spirit for awareness and intangible qualities to go to work. It's not that my husband or I are failing; we are simply being human. Operating out of our spirits, we're empowered to believe the best of one another and open space for understanding rather than judgment, blame, and division.

In closing, I have a question for you. What are you looking for in your interactions with others? Is it someone to blame or help you live a more fulfilling life? No one else is listening to your thoughts right now, so be honest with yourself about your current mindset.

Is your mindset a well-worn path? Staying on this path along the familiar route can feel safest. Are you unwilling to try a new direction or make space for anything new because it feels dangerous, untested, and would require you to change?

Is your mindset filled with the rocks of pain and woundedness from your past? Do you believe you can't let go of that pain because it is protecting you? If so, it will be difficult to allow what we have discussed in this book to take root in your life; it will be improbable for light to pierce dark places. But if you are willing to recognize the foolishness of expecting a different result without changing your thoughts and actions, choosing curiosity will propel you into trying something new.

Maybe your mindset is that you are quite willing and interested in trying this new material, but you are prone to giving up when you mess up or things don't quickly work out just how you think they should. I can assure you this path is not without turns and obstacles. Why? This information applies to most people most of the time. It does not objectify people nor guarantee that everyone will respond the same way. Please don't let the imperfection of life and the stumbles you encounter dissuade you from standing strong against misunderstanding. Let the children around you be a reminder that falling is just part of learning how to walk and continuing to get better at it. Don't let setbacks formulate a mindset that responds, *This isn't working. I tried. Forget it.*

Is your mindset hungry and open to receiving whatever will help you have better results, responses, and relationships across the spectrum of your life? By now, you understand this will require you to dig, learn, grow, and change. Instead of blaming and waiting for everyone else to change, own that you are the one who can change your world by changing your perspective. You don't have to wait on anyone else for that to happen.

You only need a willingness to dig deep, examining how you are contributing to the results in your life. Then, from what you find, keep what is life-affirming and let go of what isn't. This will position you to live and grow from abundance.

My hope is you *Don't Let Misunderstanding Win!*

About the Author

Born in Canada, Diane Lawbaugh met and married a handsome American, who remains her favorite human after four-plus decades. Diane is an international best-selling author, a graduate of Westervelt College, a professional administrator, an event planner, a singer, and a lover of all things purple.

Diane's joy is connecting people with hope, one another, and a better quality of life. To support this passion, she achieved her facilitator certification with Theotherapy, Sozo, and Heart Sync. Most recently, she added her Mastery and Certification training with PAX Programs Inc., investing over 1,300 hours in research, training, and teaching to help men and women appreciate their differences rather than see those differences as obstacles.

In 2020, Diane published her first book, *Connecting...the present to the past to find hope for your future*. She is a contributing author in the international bestsellers, *Miracle Mindset* (2022) and *Unshakable* (2024). All available on Amazon.

Diane's ideas of fun are long walks, couch picnics with her husband, romantic comedies, and all things NFL—especially cheering for her Tennessee Titans.

You can reach her at diane@hopewithoutlimits.com.

www.ingramcontent.com/pod-product-compliance
Lightning Source LLC
Chambersburg PA
CBHW062129020426
42335CB00013B/1159